How To Use This Study Guide

This ten-lesson study guide corresponds to *"The Sons of Issachar" With Rick Renner and Guests Todd Coconato, Alan DiDio, Joseph Z, Gabe Poirot, Dr. Frederick Price, Mike Signorelli, Philip Renner, Joel Renner, Ryan Edberg, and Ben Diaz* (Renner TV). Each lesson in this study guide covers a topic that is addressed during the program series, with questions and references supplied to draw you deeper into your own private study of the Scriptures on this subject.

To derive the most benefit from this study guide, consider the following:

First, watch or listen to the program prior to working through the corresponding lesson in this guide. (Programs can also be viewed at **renner.org** by clicking on the Media/Archives links or on our Renner Ministries YouTube channel.)

Second, take the time to look up the scriptures included in each lesson. Prayerfully consider their application to your own life.

Third, use a journal or notebook to make note of your answers to each lesson's Study Questions and Practical Application challenges.

Fourth, invest specific time in prayer and in the Word of God to consult with the Holy Spirit. Write down the scriptures or insights He reveals to you.

Finally, take action! Whatever the Lord tells you to do according to His Word, do it.

For added insights on this subject, it is recommended that you obtain Todd Coconato's book *Come Out From Among Them,* Joseph Z's books *Breaking Hell's Economy* and *Servants of Fire,* Mike Signorelli's book *From Chaos to Clarity,* Dr. Frederick Price's book *Behind the Seen,* Alan DiDio's book *Summoning the Demon,* Gabe Poirot's book *Built Different,* Philip Renner's book *A Fasted Life,* Ryan Edberg's book *Does God Still Heal Today?,* and Ben Diaz's book *Supernatural Healing of the Soul.* You may also select from Rick's other available resources by placing your order at **renner.org** or by calling 1-800-742-5593.

One of Rick Renner's guests during this series is Todd Coconato, founder of Todd Coconato Ministries. Todd is a pastor, national speaker, and TV and radio host who ministers to believers in the U.S. and beyond. He lives in Nashville, TN, with his wife and daughter. For more information, visit **toddcoconato.com**.

One of Rick Renner's guests during this series is Alan DiDio, founder of Encounter Ministries based in Charlotte, NC. Alan is a best-selling author, podcast host, and YouTuber who boldly teaches the Word of God, reaching millions of people around the world with the Gospel of Jesus Christ. He and his wife are the proud parents of two children. For more information, visit **encountertoday.com**.

One of Rick Renner's guests during this series is Joseph Z, founder of Z Ministries. Joseph is an international prophetic voice who builds lives by the Word of God in the church, government, and marketplace. He and his wife Heather currently reside in Colorado Springs, CO, with their two children. For more information, visit **josephz.com**.

One of Rick Renner's guests during this series is Gabe Poirot, a young, powerful voice in the Body of Christ. Gabe is a speaker, content creator, consultant, and author who preaches the Gospel on several social-media platforms. He and his wife Ally are committed to bringing the good news of God's power and love to the next generation. For more information, visit **gabepoirot.com**.

One of Rick Renner's guests during this series is Dr. Frederick Price, lead pastor of Crenshaw Christian Center in Los Angeles, CA. Dr. Price leads the congregation, teaching generations of believers the Word of God in a reverent and relatable way. He and his wife Angel are the proud parents of three children. For more information, visit **crenshawchristiancenter.net**.

One of Rick Renner's guests during this series is Mike Signorelli, lead pastor and founder of V1 Church, one of the fastest growing churches in America. Mike is passionate about empowering people to be all they were made to be. He and his wife Julie currently reside in New York City with their two daughters. For more information, visit **v1.church**.

One of Rick Renner's guests during this series is Philip Renner, a worship leader, evangelist, revivalist, and award-winning songwriter. Philip leads worship in capitols and city halls across America and boldly declares the

A Note From Rick Renner

I am on a personal quest to see a "revival of the Bible" so people can establish their lives on a firm foundation that will stand strong and endure the test as end-time storm winds begin to intensify.

In order to experience a revival of the Bible in your personal life, it is important to take time each day to read, receive, and apply its truths to your life. James tells us that if we will continue in the perfect law of liberty — refusing to be forgetful hearers, but determined to be doers — we will be blessed in our ways. As you watch or listen to the programs in this series and work through this corresponding study guide, I trust you will search the Scriptures and allow the Holy Spirit to help you hear something new from God's Word that applies specifically to your life. I encourage you to be a doer of the Word He reveals to you. Whatever the cost, I assure you — it will be worth it.

> Thy words were found, and I did eat them;
> and thy word was unto me the joy and rejoicing of mine heart:
> for I am called by thy name, O Lord God of hosts.
> — Jeremiah 15:16

Your brother and friend in Jesus Christ,

Rick Renner

The Sons of Issachar

Copyright © 2025 by Rick Renner
1814 W. Tacoma St.
Broken Arrow, OK 74012-1406

Published by Rick Renner Ministries
www.renner.org

ISBN 13: 978-1-6675-1150-4

eBook ISBN 13: 978-1-6675-1151-1

Gospel without fear in places where sin abounds. He and his wife Ella live near Atlanta, GA, with their two children. For more information, visit **philiprenner.com**.

One of Rick Renner's guests during this series is Joel Renner, the CEO of RENNER Ministries. Joel has faithfully worked alongside his father Rick Renner in nearly every aspect of the ministry, and he brings his practical insight to everything he does. Joel and his wife Olya reside in Moscow, Russia, with their two sons Mark and Daniel. For more information, visit **renner.org**.

One of Rick Renner's guests during this series is Ryan Edberg, founder of the Kingdom Movement and a respected leader and consultant in the world of event-based entertainment and Christian music. Ryan manages several organizations that aim to engage believers with worship and the Word of God. He and his wife Jenny reside in Nashville, TN, with their four children. For more information, visit **ryanedbergministries.com**.

One of Rick Renner's guests during this series is Ben Diaz, founder and lead pastor of Vida Church. Ben has traveled throughout the U.S., Mexico, and Central America leading worship and teaching the Word of God since he was 18 years old. He and his wife Kara now live in Mesa, AZ, pastoring their church and parenting their five children. For more information, visit **vidachurchaz.com**.

LESSON 1

TOPIC

Come Out From Among Them

SYNOPSIS

The ten lessons in this study titled *The Sons of Issachar* will focus on the following topics:

- Come Out From Among Them
- Breaking Hell's Economy
- From Chaos to Clarity

- Behind the Seen
- Summoning the Demon
- Built Different
- A Fasted Life
- Does God Still Heal Today?
- Supernatural Healing of the Soul
- Servants of Fire

In this program, special guest Todd Coconato shares from his book *Come Out From Among Them*, warning believers of the harmful influence culture and the entertainment industry are having on the Church. After working as a child actor in Hollywood and seeing firsthand how many well-known stars lived their lives, Todd had an encounter with the Lord that led him out of that broken world system. He now speaks boldly, calling believers to take their rightful place as the Church and become the influential people of God they were always meant to be.

As Todd and the other "sons of Issachar" ministers share, you will be emboldened to stand up and push back the presence of darkness around you. You will see that you not only have everything you need in the Word of God, but you have an anointing from the Holy Spirit that the enemy can't contend with. This is a lesson you do not want to miss!

The emphasis of this lesson:

We're living in a time when culture is actively trying to invade the Church, and it will if the Body of Christ does not stand up and stop it. While there are real powers of evil trying to take ground and intimidate the Church, there is also a blessing of supernatural protection and provision that will come to those who stand for God. Although the world is getting darker around us, as believers we have the authority to push that darkness back and to shine even brighter. This is not a time for the Church to faint or grow weary; it is a time for the Church to be prepared and boldly stand for God.

The Times in Which We Are Living

We are living in an exciting time in history. Although there are many tumultuous events occurring in the world around us, it is a truly exciting time to be alive and see what God is doing (and will continue to do) through His Church. But what is happening in the world? Why are people fearful and upset?

There are many countries around the world that are experiencing economic hardship, social and civil unrest, and even the threat of war. And the U.S. is not exempt. There are issues of economic and social concern that are escalating here as well, and that includes the possibility of civil unrest.

But Todd Coconato shared an interesting perspective in the program. He said, "There are a lot of destabilizing things that are happening right now.... I think a lot of it is induced by the powers that be, the ones behind the curtain. It's kind of what they want to have happening right now."

Todd recalled, "One of the arguments that people always try to figure out about Hollywood is, does Hollywood show the culture or is Hollywood guiding the culture with predictive programming, and I tend to think it's the second. I think that they predictively plant seeds in our minds to kind of coerce our thought processes."

Todd also mentioned there is a pattern of behavior that many people of influence seem to have followed that matches the ideology of the Cloward-Piven strategy, which you can read about in Todd's book *Come Out From Among Them*. The effect of the actions of these extremist groups and influential people have created polarization even in the Church.

Regardless of where it is coming from, most will agree that there is a lot of civil unrest in the United States, and it has created a polarized environment. Instead of the Church being the one to influence culture, it is the culture that has been influencing the Church for the last 30 years. But enough is enough — it is time for the Church to start influencing the culture again.

The Culture of the Western World

So, you might ask, where are we as a culture? Joseph Z offered that in the West, people are succumbing to an antichrist spirit. Although the Antichrist has not made himself known yet, this spiritual presence has begun to seduce people across the western world, enticing them to cooperate with its hidden agenda and bring its evil mandate throughout the land.

But there is something we can do! We can take a stand against this antichrist spirit by recognizing who we are and doing what God has called us to do. Remember, as believers we are the *ekklesia* — Christ's anointed Church — and we have been given everything we need to stand against the powers of darkness.

More specifically in the U.S., there is something else occurring. Mike Signorelli shared that in New York City, where he is from, he has observed a culture-shift toward secular humanism, or a secular humanist worldview. And as with most things, once this happens in New York City, it is almost certainly going to happen in the rest of the United States too.

People with this way of thinking have decidedly "deleted" God and religion from their worldview, so they think that instead of serving God, they are serving themselves. But the reality is, they are not serving themselves, they are serving Satan. Mike said, "As believers, we know there are only two sides, and right now the great deception is people think they're living for themselves, fulfilling their own desires, but they're cooperating with that demonic agenda."

Two other widespread issues we're seeing are the destruction of the nuclear family and confusion in gender identity. While gender confusion used to be relegated to major cities, it has now infiltrated nearly every home in the U.S. due to the Internet, and it's even happening globally. It seems clear that in the U.S., and in much of the western world, we are living in a post-Christian nation.

Aside from these significant spiritual and social issues, there are also people operating behind the scenes in an effort to create and direct some of these shifts we're experiencing in our culture. One of these groups is the World Economic Forum, which Todd also wrote about in his book. This group of leaders, people in business, and those in positions of power and influence gather to discuss what they want to happen in the world. But one thing they have discovered is the greatest restraining force that has come against their wicked plans is Spirit-filled Christians.

This exemplifies what Paul wrote in Ephesians 6:12, "For we wrestle not against flesh and blood, but against principalities, against powers, against the rulers of the darkness of this world, against spiritual wickedness in high places." And it affirms that as the Church, we are *the Great Restrainer* (*see* 2 Thessalonians 2:7).

The World Economic Forum has discovered that the Spirit-empowered Church, or people who are operating in the gifts of the Spirit, are indeed a restraining force that they can't overcome. And because of this, this sinister group is trying to scheme a way to infiltrate and restrain the Church, but nothing they have tried has been successful.

None of these things should come as a shock to us. As the apostle John said in First John 2:18, we are in the last hour, and the spirit of the antichrist is here. We are living in a time when the Church has been infiltrated by a spirit of deception, and we need to know what to do.

It is shocking to see what is happening in the western world and the United States of America. We really are living in delusionary times. The world around us is getting darker and the hearts of men are growing cold just as the Bible said they would in Matthew 24:12, but it is not time for the Church to grow weary. We must remember who we are and resolve to do what God has called us to do so that we can shine brighter and brighter in these last days.

How Do We Respond?

So what do we do? How do we respond to the state of our culture and the times in which we are living? When asked this question, Todd answered, "We need to hear from the Lord. We need to get back to His Word and back to the main thing."

Well, you might be wondering, what is the "main thing"? It is the *Great Commission*, and it is recorded in Matthew 28:19 and 20: "Go ye therefore, and teach all nations, baptizing them in the name of the Father, and of the Son, and of the Holy Ghost: teaching them to observe all things whatsoever I have commanded you: and, lo, I am with you alway, even unto the end of the world. Amen." Believers in the Body of Christ need to get back to the basics of reading and teaching the Word of God, equipping the saints, and making disciples. This is still of utmost importance to the Lord.

The Church also needs to teach people to have discernment. Several ministers on the program recommended Todd's book as an "instruction manual" for developing the tool of discernment, but you can also grow in your ability to discern by practicing listening for and responding to the voice of the Holy Spirit.

In order to navigate the stormy seas ahead of the Church, every believer must grow in his own understanding of the Bible, his personal prayer life, and his ability to discern what is of God and what is not. One way Todd and Rick said you can practice discernment is that the next time you feel a "check" in your spirit, or when you feel something is not right, ask the Holy Spirit, "Is this you?" And wait for Him to respond. He will likely say, "Yes, this is Me," or "No, this is not Me."

Each of these things will equip you to come out from among the Babylonian system that is trying to oppose God and suppress the Church. It is time for you to unite with the Lord, rise up in faith and boldness, and say to the powers of darkness, "No, I'm not moving. *You move.*" And when you do, you will begin to see victory!

Our Finest Hour Is Ahead!

On the program, Rick asked each minister what they believe might happen in the next decade in western culture and in the Church.

Alan DiDio declared that spiritually we can predict, regardless of what happens politically or socially, *if the Church returns to its roots, it wins.* First John 4:4 says, "…Greater is he that is in you, than he that is in the world," and that verse is actually referring to an antichrist spirit. If the Church will recognize that there is a Spirit in us who is greater than this antichrist spirit in the world, we will begin to see unity in the Church like we've never seen it before.

Although there will certainly be darkness in the next ten years, Alan said that for the Church, "This will be our finest hour." Psalm 91 is going to become a reality for every single believer, and there will be a remnant that will rise up and be victorious in this hour.

Several ministers agreed that in the coming years we will likely see droughts and economic decline in parts of the U.S., and Alan even predicted we will see a fracturing of states in the United States of America. He stated that certain states will come under judgment because of their decisions to move away from godly principles. On the other hand, we will likely see several states that choose to embrace godly principles prosper and be blessed.

While the judgment on some states will appear obvious, Mike Signorelli also warned that in the midst of this we may see the unrighteous claim a counterfeit, or false, blessing — something that looks like it's from God but is not. This is one important reason why we need wisdom more than ever for the days ahead. We can't simply be guided by what we see or hear in the News and media or by what other people around us say. We must be led by the Spirit and learn to accurately discern and hear what is happening in this hour.

Fred Price added that this will be a time when it is more obvious who is a child of God and who is a *son* of God (*see* Romans 8:14). It's also an opportunity for the Church to return to the example of the Church we see in the book of Acts, where there was no lack among them, there was unity, and the Lord added to their number daily. Rick agreed and said that while we see the world returning to paganism, we are seeing the Church return to the example outlined in the book of Acts. In the next several years, what's happening in the world will likely get darker, but it will in turn serve as fuel for believers to run back to God's original plan for the Church.

God is always looking at the hearts of men. And in these last days, we need to ask ourselves whether we are serving ourselves or serving the Lord. Todd suggested, instead of asking God, "What can you do for me?," ask Him, "What can I do for you, Lord?" When we position ourselves that way, the favor and anointing of God is on us and we will be unstoppable no matter what power of darkness comes against us.

Every day with God is an adventure, and as we walk in these uncertain times, we must remember that as believers we are not in the same boat as everyone else. We are protected in God; we are in His ark of safety. Even if the economy were to fail or falter, we are in the economy of God. And while there is real darkness and evil in the world, as we are faithful to seek the Lord, spend time in His Word, and practice hearing His voice, we will have everything we need to sail above the storms that are ahead.

STUDY QUESTIONS

Study to shew thyself approved unto God, a workman that needeth not to be ashamed, rightly dividing the word of truth.
— 2 Timothy 2:15

1. Alan DiDio declared that spiritually we can predict, regardless of what happens politically or socially, that if the Church returns to its roots, it wins. What are our roots? Read the following verses while answering this question.
   • Joshua1:8

- Psalm 19:7-11
- Psalm 119:105
- Matthew 4:4
- John 1:1
- John 17:17
- Romans 10:17
- Second Timothy 3:16 and 17
- Hebrews 4:12

2. When discussing where we are as a culture, Joseph Z mentioned that in the West, people are succumbing to an antichrist spirit. Although the Antichrist has not made himself known yet, this spiritual presence has begun to seduce people across the Western world, enticing them to cooperate with its hidden agenda and bring its evil mandate throughout the land. We are living in a time when the Church has been infiltrated by a spirit of deception (the spirit of the Antichrist), and we need to know what to do. According to what we discussed in this lesson, what are some ways we can prepare for and resist the spirit of the Antichrist? Consider the following verses on the spirit of Antichrist and the spirit of deception:

- 1 John 4:2 and 3
- 2 Corinthians 11:13-15; 2 Thessalonians 2:3; 1 John 2:18-22; and 2 John 7
- Jude 4-18

PRACTICAL APPLICATION

But be ye doers of the word, and not hearers only,
deceiving your own selves.
—James 1:22

1. In order to navigate the stormy seas ahead of the Church, every believer must grow in his own understanding of the Bible, his personal prayer life, and his ability to discern what is of God and what is not. One way Todd and Rick said you can practice discernment is that the next time you feel a "check" in your spirit, or when you feel something is not right, ask the Holy Spirit, "Is this You?" Have you ever

had a "check" in your spirit and ignored it only to later realize that if you had listened, you wouldn't have to deal with the mess you were currently in? Have you had an experience of listening to a check and being glad you did? What are some ways you can practice listening to this internal voice more regularly and accurately?

2. Todd Coconato talked about how we as believers need to return to God's Word and the "main thing," which is the Great Commission. Take some time to read through Jesus' Great Commission to us in Matthew 28:19 and 20. Have you been doing any of the actions listed in these verses? If not, what is something you can do to change that?

NOTES

Todd Coconato. *Come Out From Among Them*. Lake Mary, FL: Charisma House, 2023.

LESSON 2

TOPIC

Breaking Hell's Economy

SYNOPSIS

In this riveting lesson, Joseph Z takes the lead to share from his book *Breaking Hell's Economy*. He explains that to break the hold hell's economy has on our life, we need a revelation of how that entire system and culture operates. Instead of following what the news says or copying what we see our neighbor do, we need to open the Word of God for ourselves and discover what God has asked us to do with our money and how to posture our hearts. If we want to break free from hell's economy, we must trust that what God says is true and put His Word to the test.

As the "sons of Issachar" discuss this fascinating topic, you will gain a deeper understanding about finances, giving, the wealth of Jesus, the spirit of poverty, tithing, and so much more. In this lesson, we will see, again, that if the Church will remember who it is and all that has been made available in Jesus, there won't be any power of hell that can stand against it. Hell has its own economy and way of functioning, but so does Heaven — and as believers, we need to know what that is.

The emphasis of this lesson:

Many believers are held captive by a deceptive way of thinking that says God wants them to be poor, but that is a lie. As Joseph Z opens this topic about hell's economy, you will discover that God not only wants to provide for you, but He wants to provide such an abundant blessing that it breaks the yoke of any bondage in your life. He doesn't just want you to exist in this broken world, He wants you to succeed and live as an example of His extravagant love.

A Vow of Poverty

While there are many issues opposing the Church from outside its doors, there are also certain mindsets within its walls that have kept it crippled and ineffective. One of those such mindsets is believing that Christians must be poor to serve God.

Alan DiDio said it best as he stated on the program, "I really feel like the Body of Christ needs to get a divorce from the poverty spirit. We need to break our vow of poverty that we have made in the Body of Christ."

To do what God has called us to do and to stand up against the kingdom of darkness, we must break away from this mindset and the broken system that tells us it is more holy to serve God when we barely have enough to get by. Instead of agreeing with the economy of hell, we need to lean into the economy of Heaven and allow God to operate in our lives the way He longs to.

The Economy of Hell

So how do we do this? First, we need to understand what the economy of hell is. The economy of hell, or the Luciferian economy, is founded on the spirit of mammon, also known as the spirit of selfishness, which at its root is the love of money. It is called the Luciferian economy because before Satan fell from Heaven, his name was Lucifer. And after he had been put in charge of all the commerce in the world, overseeing God's glory, he fell in love with money. Greed and pride entered his heart, and he became jealous of God. That's why he fell from his position, and the Luciferian economy still tempts man the same way.

In Second Corinthians 4:4, Paul called Satan the "god of this world," and the Greek word he used for "world" is the word *kosmos*, which describes *ordered systems*. This does not mean Satan is the god of the *earth*. Paul wrote it to describe how the enemy operates. He doesn't have any anointing of his own, so he has to work through world systems and economies, manipulating ordered things — society, culture, and money, for example, — like puppets in his hands.

It is interesting to observe that in Scripture, we see several examples of people who sought to control and manipulate commerce or money just like the enemy does. Cain and Abel fought over an offering, Judas Iscariot was in control of the purse among Jesus' disciples, and the Antichrist is described as one who will control the world economy one day. Each of these instances reveals that the same spirit, the spirit of mammon and the love of money, is indeed behind the way the economy of hell operates.

How the Magi Broke Hell's Economy

So what biblical examples do we have of people who broke free of hell's economy? One powerful example is the Magi who broke the grip of hell's economy over Jesus right after He was born. The Magi were an elite, powerful, fabulously wealthy group of high-ranking priests who were devoted to studying dreams and the stars. They carried so much esteem and political clout that they were viewed as *king-makers* in Eastern lands. And, interestingly, the first biblical connection of the Magi began with Daniel.

After Daniel was taken to Babylon in about 600 BC, many scholars believe he became the head of the Magi. They revered his faith, prophecies, and the Scriptures he treasured so much that this elite group believed in and were waiting for the Messiah to be born. As they diligently studied the stars, they were directed to the place where Jesus was, and they brought Him multitudes of gifts.

In Rick's book *Christmas — The Rest of the Story*, he provides a catalog of gifts the Magi historically would have brought to a king of very high-ranking status. But they were traveling to honor the King of kings, the most powerful king the world had ever seen, so we can assume it was likely even more than that.

Joseph Z shared on the program that he believes God used these gifts from the Magi to provide for Jesus and His family and to later finance

Jesus' ministry. He said, "They [the Magi] broke the devil's hold over Him [Jesus] financially. Now…if God were sending His Son, or if any one of us sent our children to do an assignment, I don't think we'd want to send them empty-handed or say, 'Figure it out. You're on your own.' God sent Jesus and then He said, 'You know what? You're my Son in whom I'm well pleased.' But He proved it even when Jesus was young. He financed the whole picture."

The Magi brought Jesus their best, and because of their abundant gifts and treasures, Jesus was well supplied from the very beginning of His life. Philippians 4:19 says, "But my God shall supply all your need…," and in reference to this verse, Rick added, "I believe the arrival of the Magi is such a demonstration of that verse. God sent His Son into the earth to do a major mission, and He financed it from His birth." God provided for His Son abundantly so that He would have everything He needed to accomplish His assignment on the earth.

And when Jesus died, it seems that His wealth did not just disappear. Shortly after Jesus' death and burial, Joseph of Arimathea became the wealthiest man in the region. Some speculate that this is because the wealth of Jesus was transferred to him after Jesus' died. There is also a strong argument that Joseph of Arimathea was Jesus' uncle, which would explain why Jesus was buried in his tomb. Although there is no way to know for certain, it is interesting to think about.

How Do We Live in This Economy?

The Bible says that as believers we live in this world, but we are not of this world (*see* John 17:16), so how do we live in this world that operates with an economy we do not belong to?

Joseph Z offered that if you don't want the spirit of mammon to have a choke hold on you, you need to be a radical giver. That is a surefire way to break the grip of hell's economy on your life. Another way to approach it is to recognize there are three steps to experience breakthrough, and this is outlined for us in Isaiah 10:27:

> **And it shall come to pass in that day, that his burden shall be taken away from off thy shoulder, and his yoke from off thy neck, and the yoke shall be destroyed because of the anointing.**

In context, this verse describes people breaking free of political oppression, and the same three steps apply to breaking free of hell's economy. First, the anointing *lifts* the yoke off the shoulders, then it will *loose* the yoke off the neck, and finally it will *destroy* the yoke.

The word for "anointing" in this verse actually describes the muscularity or fatness of the neck. It pictures an ox that begins to grow so muscular and strong that it outgrows the yoke so it can no longer hold it. This illustrates exactly what the anointing of God does in our lives. When believers go to a ministry meeting, often they will feel lighter and freer, and they will recognize that God is doing something in their life. But they stop too soon. They thank the Lord and go home thinking they have had breakthrough, but in reality, it was just getting started.

Breakthrough is not complete until you move through what is weighing you down and you are completely delivered from what's been containing you. In other words, it's not done until financially, physically, mentally, emotionally, everything begins to flow the way God intended for it to flow from the beginning. And as Joseph said in the program, if the Church will understand this and work toward that kind of breakthrough together, we could become the number one superpower in the world!

How Do We Become Radical Givers?

Mike Signorelli mentioned the example of the rich young ruler in Mark 10. He said, "The problem [with the rich young ruler] wasn't that he had properties. It was that the properties had him.... There are people listening right now who are saying, 'I just can't do that. They don't know my situation,' but the whole point is that radical generosity is what breaks that yoke of bondage." Then Mike made another powerful statement: "In times like this, everyone is going to hoard up because that is part of Satan's economy, to store up. But God gives seed to the sower. So it's not about what you have, it's about what you sow."

This demonstrates the powerful principle of sowing and reaping. When we cooperate with the economy of Heaven, following this biblical principle, the blessing and favor of God comes on us and breaks that yoke of bondage on our lives.

One example of radical giving in the Bible is when Mary took expensive ointment and anointed Jesus, extravagantly pouring it on Him and wiping His feet with her hair (*see* John 12:3). Her lavish display of love for the

Lord was a radical gift that broke hell's economy, but it also caused Judas Iscariot to manifest. In verse 5, we read that he became offended and said, "Why was not this ointment sold for three hundred pence, and given to the poor?" But the Bible tells us in the next verse that he didn't even care about the poor. He just wanted the money for himself.

Mary's example shows us what one radical gift can do when we put what we have into the hands of Jesus. But it also warns us that when any extravagant gift is given, critics are likely to appear.

In the program, Mike gave this word of caution: "We're living in a time when radical generosity is going to cause Judas to manifest in the Body of Christ." What he meant is that when believers begin to give radically, it will expose those in the Church who are in agreement with that same spirit of mammon, like Judas was, because they will become critical and say things like, "Why wasn't that money used for something else? How could you give such a large sum of money? Don't you care how that makes other people feel?" But that way of thinking is not of God. It is the thinking of the economy of hell.

Breaking Free From Poverty

Similar to this critical spirit that is prevalent in the Body of Christ, many Christians have a problem believing that God wants His children to prosper. People have an issue even hearing that Jesus was wealthy instead of poor, but in Matthew 10:9 Jesus told His disciples not to take gold, silver, or brass with them in their money belts. Why would Jesus tell them not to take gold, silver, and brass with them if they didn't have it to begin with? And just think about it. Jesus was so well provided for, even while Judas stole money from their supply, there was still enough to sustain the disciples and their ministry.

Satan has lied to the Body of Christ, telling us that Jesus was poor therefore the Church should be poor. But that's what it is — a *lie*. The enemy has sold this deception to believers to keep the Church broke, poor, and ineffective, but the truth is, if the people of God will look at what the Gospel has to say about prosperity, it speaks for itself. When Jesus talked about money in His parables, He always used big, massive sums of money. There are no small examples that Jesus uses.

But regardless, the temptation to hang on to what we have is still there. Recent statistics show that at the time of this writing giving has decreased in the U.S., and it is likely the same in other parts of the world as well. The times in which we are living are tempting us to hoard what we have, boasting that it is right to think purely analytically and logically, but, again, that is the thinking of hell's economy. To break free from this spirit of poverty, we must choose to step into the realm of the Spirit where there is true life and abundance.

God wants to break you out! He wants to set you free so that you can succeed and thrive no matter what is happening in the world around you. Just imagine what would have happened if the rich young ruler had obeyed Jesus and sold all his possessions to give his money to the poor. If he would have done the difficult, Jesus would have done the *impossible*.

We can't quantify what God wants to do in our lives through our giving. It's not about having a perfect formula where what we give will exactly measure out a certain response from God. As Todd Coconato stated in the program, God owns the cattle on a thousand hills (*see* Psalm 50:10), and there is no lack in the Lord (Psalm 34:10). He doesn't need our money. What He's really after is getting us to participate in the *economy of Heaven*, using the biblical principles written in His Word. And when we do, we will begin to see that we can never outgive God. No matter how big a gift or how great a sacrifice we give, God will always reciprocate, giving His blessing, favor, protection, and provision to us in an even more abundant way.

What About Tithing?

When the subject of giving or money comes up, one of the questions people ask most often is whether or not tithing was for the Old Testament only. To answer this question, Joseph Z quoted Hebrews 7:8 (*NKJV*), which says:

Here mortal men receive tithes, but there he receives them, of whom it is witnessed that he lives.

Joseph went on to say, "Looking at this, you don't *have* to tithe. You *get* to. I don't think it's a hard and fast rule. I don't think it's a Heaven or hell issue, but I do believe, in the New Testament, that if you do that [tithe], you are going above and beyond. I think you're stepping into something that's got some hot sauce on it."

What Joseph was saying is, when you tithe, there is a principle at work. When you take faith-filled action in the natural realm, there is a supernatural reaction in the spirit realm. It is the here and there principle — *here* mortal men receive tithes, but *there*, in the spirit realm, he receives them. As we activate this biblical principle, it unlocks something profound in the spirit. It bursts shackles, it opens doors, it rebukes the devourer, and it opens to us a new covenant, a better promise.

Dr. Frederick Price offered a different opinion. Although his perspective is a little different than Joseph's, he still believes we as Christians are called to be givers and sowers. He quoted Second Corinthians 9:6, saying, "If you sow sparingly, you reap sparingly. If you sow bountifully, you reap bountifully." He also importantly added, "I believe it's not only about what you sow, but *how* you sow is how you reap…. Anytime we sow we should be looking beyond 30-, 60-, and 100-fold. We should be looking for the manifold return on whatever it is that we sow. As people of God, as believers in the Lord, and as part of the Lord's Church here in the earth realm, I believe giving is not just something that we do every once in a while, but we should be living a *lifestyle* of giving. It's a good work that we should constantly be walking in."

This is why giving is so important. Whether or not we believe tithing is for the New Testament, giving generously activates the Kingdom of God. When we give, we participate in the economy of Heaven and open the door to God's blessing and supply in our lives. And according to Galatians 6:7, the consistency of our sowing will determine the consistency of our reaping.

Generosity Breaks Hell's Economy

Joel Renner said, "God is a multiplier. He will multiply what you give Him. And we need to copy what He does as much as we can." This is beautifully illustrated for us in the record of Jesus feeding the 5,000. John 6:9 tells us Jesus took five small barley loaves and two small fish from a boy and fed the entire crowd of more than 5,000 that was with Him. The Greek word used here is the word *krithinos*, which describes *a barley cracker*, meaning the food this boy was carrying consisted of five crackers and two small fish. Jesus fed an entire crowd with a small snack!

It may be easy to become discouraged about what you have to give, but the truth is, if everyone gave what they had, it would really make a huge difference. As long as what we have remains in our own hands, it will stay small. But the moment we put our small portion into God's hands, it will *multiply, it will break hell's economy!*

A lot of people say you can't outgive God, but most people never try. God wants us to put His Word to the test so we can see firsthand that what His Word says is true. If we give generously to God, giving Him what is first and what is best from our supply, He will respond. Our giving will be a sweet-smelling savor to Him (*see* Philippians 4:18), and as He catches wind of it, His presence will say, "I'm coming down to where that gift has been given. I want to see what that is."

This is exactly what we see God do with Solomon in First Kings 3. Solomon dedicated the Temple and gave a generous number of sacrifices. Then the Lord visited him in a dream and said, "What do you want? Ask, and I will give it to you!" (v.5). That is the kind of giving that breaks hell's economy. And if the Church can receive a revelation of this principle of giving, it will be *unstoppable*. There won't be a barrier or obstacle it can't break through.

At the end of the program, Joseph Z said, "When we stand up in faith, the devil might come walking over, but he will go limping back because the Spirit of God that is in us will open up every good and perfect gift to us." He went on to say, "God has not anointed us to lose; He's anointed us to win. This is straight from the Word of God.... We've all been there in that place of not enough where we don't have what we need. I just believe God says, 'If you'll just exchange some faith with me and take an action of faith, whether it's giving or obedience, or whatever it might be, you'll begin to outgrow the yoke.' God wants you to win even more than you do. He *delights* in you winning; He takes no glory in your failure or your brokenness or any of it. He wants you to win!" These promises are for you, and they are straight from the Word of God.

In the next lesson, we'll hear from Mike Signorelli and learn about how to find clarity in the midst of a culture steeped in chaos.

STUDY QUESTIONS

Study to shew thyself approved unto God, a workman that needeth not to be ashamed, rightly dividing the word of truth.
— 2 Timothy 2:15

1. In this lesson, we discussed how the Magi broke hell's economy over Jesus right after He was born by financing His earthly ministry. According to what you learned in this lesson, who were the Magi?

What were the gifts they gave to Jesus? Have you ever thought to consider what happened to those luxurious gifts after they were given? Read Matthew 2:1-12 with the new perspective given in this lesson.

2. In Scripture, we see several examples of people who sought to control and manipulate commerce or money just like the enemy does. Cain and Abel fought over an offering, Judas Iscariot was in control of the purse among Jesus' disciples, and the Antichrist is described as one who will control the world economy one day. Each of these instances reveals that the same spirit, the spirit of mammon and the love of money, is indeed behind the way the economy of hell operates. According to this lesson, what are some ways believers can combat the choke hold the love of money has over them? Consider the following verses that warn against the love of money:

- Ecclesiastes 5:10

- Matthew 6:24

- Mark 10:23-27

- Luke 16:13-15

- First Timothy 3:3

- First Timothy 6:9-11

- Second Timothy 3:1-5

- Hebrews 13:5 (*AMPC*)

3. According to Joseph Z, there are three steps to break hell's economy over yourself found in Isaiah 10:27. What are the steps we should take to break the love of mammon's hold over our lives?

PRACTICAL APPLICATION

But be ye doers of the word, and not hearers only,
deceiving your own selves.
—James 1:22

1. Within the Church, it is widely believed that Christians must be poor to serve God. But that's what it is — a *lie*. The enemy has sold this deception to believers to keep the Church broke, poor, and ineffective, but the truth is, if the people of God will look at what the Gospel has to say about prosperity, it speaks for itself. The problem isn't that we have properties; the problem is when we let our properties have us.

Have you allowed financial worries and obsessions to become an idol in your life, even if unknowingly? If so, what are some steps you can take to break hell's hold on you? Pray and ask God to open your heart to His leading and be willing to give when He asks you to!

2. A lot of people say you can't outgive God, but most people never try. God wants us to put His Word to the test so we can see firsthand that what His Word says is true. What do you think would happen if you decided to put the promises in God's Word to the test and put to action what it says? Take some time today to look over the many promises found in the Bible and ask God for "the eyes of your understanding being enlightened; that ye may know what is the hope of his calling, and what the riches of the glory of his inheritance in the saints, and what is the exceeding greatness of his power to us-ward who believe, according to the working of his mighty power" (Ephesians 1:18,19).

NOTES

Joseph Z. *Breaking Hell's Economy — Your Guide to Last-Days Supernatural Provision.* Shippensburg, PA: Harrison House Publishers, 2022.

TOPIC

From Chaos to Clarity

SYNOPSIS

We are living in a time of great chaos. People are more confused, more medicated, more anxious, and more depressed than ever, and we often blame it on society. But the truth is, any area of disobedience in our life can produce this unwanted chaos. We can have clarity in the midst of chaos, but it requires full surrender — not 95 or 97 percent surrendered, but 100 percent.

In this eye-opening lesson, Mike Signorelli shares unique and powerful insights from his book *From Chaos to Clarity*. As he is joined by the other "sons of Issachar," Mike and the group discuss brokenness in our society and culture as well as the possibility of what could happen in our cities, our nation, and the world if believers would choose to fully surrender their lives to God. If you are hungry for a deeper revelation of how to live firmly planted on the Word of God in this late hour, this lesson is for you.

The emphasis of this lesson:

Are you experiencing the "wow" factor of God in your life? If not, you can be! As you learn to take your hands off the steering wheel and surrender yourself to be 100-percent obedient to God, you will discover that God wants to move powerfully on your behalf to set you free and reach the people in your life who don't know Him yet. We serve a living God who is passionate about reaching the lost, and He still does wonders and miracles today.

Mike Signorelli pastors the fastest-growing church in America in New York City, which gives him a unique perspective to speak to the issues in today's culture. When Rick asked Mike in the program whether things are as bad in New York City as he had heard, Mike responded, "It's worse. It's worse than what the news is covering. And for anybody who's like, 'Well, I don't live in New York City — that doesn't have anything to do with me,' the truth is, it's coming for you."

There are many situations in New York City, as well as other major cities across the U.S., unfolding right now that have been engineered by those in power, but we don't have to be afraid. The devil may have a plan, but God has a plan, too, and He is positioning key people to be right where He wants them to be. That is why it's more important than ever for believers to come into clarity about the question, "Why am I here? What is it that God is asking me to do in these last days?"

Satan's Plan vs. God's Plan

You might be wondering, *What is the devil's plan?* The devil's plan has always been to convince us to operate in pride and think things are all about us. This is not exclusive to nonbelievers; there are Christians who fall into this wrong thinking as well. And because of this, churches in America have strayed away from the Great Commission and fulfilling the assignment Jesus gave us.

Mike made a powerful statement in the program, saying, "I think the great delusion is to believe, 'I'm living my life for me,' and it has infiltrated Christianity. It's so easy to look at people in witchcraft and the occult and say, 'Oh, look how deceived they are.' But you have Christians who are controlling their own situation and their own life as well." He emphasized that the message believers need to hear is to completely and totally surrender their lives to God. It seems basic, but remember, the simplest things are often the hardest to do.

So what is God's plan? God's plan is still to commission His Church to reach the lost. *This has not changed,* and we find it in Matthew 28:18-20:

> **And Jesus came and spake unto them, saying, All power is given unto me in heaven and in earth. Go ye therefore, and teach all nations, baptizing them in the name of the Father, and of the Son, and of the Holy Ghost: Teaching them to observe all things whatsoever I have commanded you: and, lo, I am with you always, even unto the end of the world. Amen.**

Rick shared that there is a promise here that many believers do not realize. The word "lo" in verse 20 in the original language means *wow, wow, wow, this is amazing!* It would be better translated, "Will I ever be with you even to the end of the age!" It is God's guarantee to us that if we go, if we preach, or if we give to help others go reach the lost, the *wow factor* of God will show up in our churches and ministries.

There are a lot of people who say, "We just don't see the power of God in our church," or "I don't experience the power of God in my life." But the truth is, they are not doing what brings the "wow factor" of God. You must be involved in doing the Great Commission for the power of God to show up.

We often hear about signs and wonders happening in other countries, and this is why. They are actively involved in reaching the lost. If you're not experiencing the power and presence of God in your life or in your church, ask yourself, "What am I, or what is my church, doing to reach the lost?" If the answer is "nothing," there is no guarantee that God's power is going to show up. If you are not involved in reaching the lost or giving so others can go, His power will begin to dissipate from your midst.

The Miraculous Power of God

The fact that the Church has drifted away from our original assignment really seems to be one symptom of a larger problem. To see the miraculous, supernatural power of God in our lives, we must fully surrender our lives to God 100 percent.

In the program, Mike shared that in college he had been an atheist, fully relying on science, logic, and intellect as he denied the existence of God. All these years later, he pastors the fastest growing church in the U.S. where verifiable miracles happen on a weekly basis, and he described that to remain open to the miraculous happening in his church and in his life, he has to make a conscious choice to turn off his scientific mind and turn on his faith instead: "When I get into these moments where I fully surrender and I shut down that scientific mind and say the One who actually created the universe can change and break rules at his will, the miraculous just begins to happen.... I really believe it comes from a place of surrenderedness. For me, you know, God doesn't want me partially dead; He wants me totally dead."

So what does it mean to surrender our lives to God? In one capacity, it means we must starve our doubts, fears, and anxieties and choose to feed ourselves the Word of God. What we starve will die, and what we feed will grow. We must feed our faith with the Word of God and surrender our doubts and hesitations to God.

This means we can't compartmentalize what we give to Jesus. Many people think, "I'll give Jesus my heart," and that's all they ever give to Him. But the truth is, He wants your mind, your body, your money — He wants every part of you! It's not enough to give Jesus your heart. He wants so much more than that. You're not surrendered until you've come and laid the whole thing on the altar.

Todd Coconato shared that he and his wife have seen the biggest breakthroughs in their lives when they were 100 percent obedient to the Lord, not 99 percent obedient. From this we see that surrender is also about committing to be obedient to the Lord. And when you do, you will see breakthrough happen in your life.

We Are Called To Be Living Sacrifices

This decision to surrender your life to Christ and choose to be 100 percent obedient is not about doing things perfectly all the time. It is about choosing to live a lifestyle of repentance, quickly laying things at Jesus' feet and getting back on track, so that you can hear from the Lord clearly and then doing what He says.

Todd shared, "Every day I have to repent." Rick agreed and said, "That's why I get up early in the morning. I get up at about four o'clock in the morning, go get my coffee, do my push-ups, then I go in and sit in my place. The first thing I do is say, 'Alright, Lord, here I am. We're starting all over again today.'" We're to be *living sacrifices*, that's why we must come before God and lay our lives on the altar, surrendering ourselves to Him every day.

Todd went on to say, "I believe the enemy's greatest nightmare is if the Church actually utilizes the tools that we have and operates in them, if we actually do what we're called to do. And I believe that's what the Lord is doing in this hour. He's calling for a Church to rise up, as Joseph Z often says, *to stand*. You know, we've got to take a stand in this hour and push back and be that restraining force because many are the plans of the wicked, but that doesn't mean they're all going to succeed." Being surrendered isn't just about giving God our heart; it's about surrendering our lives and becoming that driving force in culture that can expel and cast out the powers of darkness. If we as believers do that, just think about what the Church is capable of doing.

Mike's Personal Testimony

In the program, Joseph Z asked Mike to share what happened in his life to bring him to this place of anointing and surrender. Mike said:

> I kept thinking, there are Levites then there are Nazarites, you know? Think about Samson. I think the call on his life was supposed to be full of surrender, but it was in his compromise that there was a loss of that anointing, that power. And so, I think what my life represents is what it would look like if there was complete and total surrender. It's like John said, 'I decrease so that you can increase.' So then if that's the equation, How much can I decrease?

I had crippling social anxiety. If you knew me as a child and a teen, sitting at this table right now would have been virtually impossible for me to talk. I would grab the glass and my hand would shake. But at 15 years old, I was reading the book of Acts, and I got to the part where Peter steps up and preaches boldly, and I actually got angry. I said, 'This guy's an idiot.' I said, 'Why Peter?' And then the Gospel clicked. That's when Acts 1:8, '…After the Holy Spirit comes on you…,' made sense. So I sat on the edge of my bed and read, 'You'll receive power to be witnesses….'

I sat on the edge of my bed at 15 years old, alone in my room, and said, 'God, if you can do it with Peter, do it with me.' And I had a personal Pentecost. It didn't happen in a church for me; it just happened in my attic bedroom, but it transformed me so radically. It was like I couldn't do it and then I could do it. It's the only explanation I have, but it really came from that moment of surrender.

There are so many believers who are sacrificing their next level of depth and anointing in God at the altar of intellectualism. But the truth is, when we say, "God, I choose to believe despite all of these thoughts and doubts," the power just flows.

When we look at the story of David in the Bible, we see that anxiety was running rampant through the minds of people around him who were listening to the taunts of Goliath. Even the military generals were panicking, but David, because he was in the secret place, had clarity and knew what to do. And when there was a famine throughout the land of Egypt, Joseph knew what to do. This shows us that in the time we're living in, when anxiety is rampant and famine is sure to come, we need clarity more than ever. And, as Mike shared in the program, clarity comes from intimacy.

What About Cessationists?

While Mike and his church experience miracles on a weekly basis, there are those who do not believe the gifts of the Holy Spirit are still in operation today. Instead, they believe the supernatural gifts of the Holy Spirit and miracles ended after the Twelve Apostles died. This is called cessationism.

Many people with this way of thinking have publicly attacked Mike and his ministry because he openly shares about the miracles, healings, and moves of the Holy Spirit they are seeing take place. Unfortunately for cessationists, the more they try to oppose and disprove that these miracles are happening, the more miracles that seem to occur.

Mike related in the program that he understands and agrees that more biblical literacy is needed in the Body of Christ, but studying the Bible does not disprove that miracles still occur today. It does the opposite. When you closely examine what Scripture says, it becomes virtually impossible to deny that the gifts of the Spirit should be in operation today.

Many people who oppose the miraculous taking place in the Body of Christ today have often had a bad experience of their own such as a time when they were hurt by someone at church, or they believed for a miracle to take place and then they were disappointed when it didn't happen. Cessationists want others to believe they are having an intellectual discussion when they argue with someone claiming to have experienced a miracle, but in fact, they are having an emotional one.

Rick made an interesting point in the program. He said, "In the First Century, paganism had signs and wonders. You could go into any pagan temple, and you could see miraculous things or prophetic events take place. If Christianity had come with no miracles, it never could have competed in that environment. It had to come with power so tremendous that the pagans would say, 'Wait, we've seen the supernatural, but we have never seen anything like this.' It really authenticated the Gospel. And we need it now. I mean, we're living in a day when people are not taking us serious, but when the power of God comes into demonstration, it changes the conversation."

The miracle-working power of God authenticates the message God has given us to bring to others. We even see this in the story of Moses in Genesis. God didn't just send Moses with good words to say to Pharaoh, he gave him power to compete with and decimate the magicians Pharaoh had. Pharaoh's magician's had power, but what God had given Moses was beyond anything Egypt had ever seen. And it is the same with us — God has given us power to do what He is asking us to do.

Mark 16:17 says, "And these signs shall follow them that *believe*...." A lot of people had faith at one time to see the supernatural occur, but they have since moved out of faith. You have to engage your faith for signs and wonders to be activated. And when you do, you will begin to see the miraculous occur.

A Fascination With the Supernatural

Although many are hungry to see the supernatural take place, often they look for ways to access it that are outside of God. On TikTok there is a hashtag called "witch talk" that has over a billion views. This is just one example of how our culture has been actively trying to normalize occult practices and witchcraft among people of every generation, not just the younger ones. And this is happening all over the world. Mike made the comment, "I do believe that we're stepping into a prophets of Baal versus Elijah moment. And it's more important than ever that we understand the fullness of what's available to us through Christ."

This is not a new occurrence either. Rick shared that he and Denise observed a similar event in the former Soviet Union. While the Soviet Union was in power, atheism reigned and religion was basically outlawed, so psychic phenomena emerged as a result. People were so hungry for the supernatural that every single morning, the nation's number one psychic came on television to speak. Rick stated, "If people don't find the answers they need in the Gospel, their hunger is going to lead them to look for it somewhere else. And we have a God-given responsibility to bring the supernaturalness of Christ to people."

As believers we need to show people who God really is and not be afraid for our presence to demand an explanation. We are living in a society that is overrun with anxiety as people obsess over the obstacles and giants in their lives, but we are called to be people whose gaze stays locked on God. In the story of David, the whole nation of Israel was gazing at Goliath, fixating on him and obsessing over his threats, but David had his gaze locked on God. He knew who he was, and because he was looking to God, not worrying about Goliath, he had clarity to know what needed to be done. His presence demanded an explanation, and so can ours when we truly know who we are in Christ.

You Don't Need a Plan B

Something Mike has realized in teaching people to understand their identity in Christ is that sometimes we have to actually destroy everything we've built and bring it down to the foundation, back to ground zero, and say, "God, now you make me into what you want to make me into." Doing this brings us to the point of clarity. It's that moment when you're able to say, "God,

I'm willing to gut it all out," and in reckless abandon you decide there's no turning back.

When an airplane is taking off, there is actually a point when the pilots take their hands off the controls as the plane comes off the runway. They calculate the length of the runway and the speed that they need to go for thrust and lift, and when pilots take their hands off, the plane actually comes off the ground. It's called the V-1, which is also the name of Mike's church. It's the point when the pilots decide the plane is going to fly. There's no turning back; there's no Plan B.

A problem many people have, even those in the Church, is that they have a Plan B, a Plan C, a Plan D, and a Plan E. But God looked at the world and said, "I have one plan. It's Jesus — it's the Great Commission," and He's asking us to do the same. He wants us to take our hands off the controls of our life and trust Him that we're going to fly. That is our point of clarity.

Later in the program, Mike said, "I believe the Church is going to rise, lacking in nothing," and this is how we get there. When we totally surrender our life to God and take our hands off the controls, saying, "I don't have a Plan B, God. Take my life and build what you want with it," He will begin to move, bringing clarity and order and purpose to our life. We will become clear conduits and channels for the power of God to move through us and reach a lost and hurting world.

STUDY QUESTIONS

Study to shew thyself approved unto God, a workman that needeth not to be ashamed, rightly dividing the word of truth.
— 2 Timothy 2:15

1. At the beginning of this lesson, we discussed what the enemy's plan for the world is versus what God's plan is. How are you participating in God's plan? Write down one or two ways you are actively involved in reaching the lost — or ways you want to be if you're not currently involved.

2. Romans 12:1 tells us we are called to be living sacrifices. Are you fully surrendered, giving your life to Jesus every day? Read this passage and reflect on what stands out to you about how to live a life fully surrendered to the Lord.

3. What are cessationists? What do they believe about the gifts of the Holy Spirit? Do you agree with this? Why or why not?

4. In this lesson, Rick shared that ancient pagan religions also operated in the supernatural. Why do you think that was significant? What do you think those ancient people thought when Christians began to lay hands on people and see the sick healed and demon-possessed people set free?

PRACTICAL APPLICATION

**But be ye doers of the word, and not hearers only,
deceiving your own selves.
—James 1:22**

1. Have you seen miracles happen in your own life? If so, write down your experience and reflect on the goodness of God. If not, write down a testimony you've heard someone else share about God working in his or her life. Take a few minutes to invite the Holy Spirit to move supernaturally in your life and expect that He will do it.

2. In what areas of your life are you quick to obey? In what areas of your life are you slow to obey? If you need to, repent and ask the Lord to forgive you in the areas where you've been disobedient. Commit to prioritize obedience in those areas of your life this week.

3. Are you the leader or pastor at your church? If so, take a moment to ask yourself whether your church is experiencing the gifts of the Spirit and the power of God. What changes could you make to invite even more of His presence to come?

4. If your life has gotten out of control, there is something you can do. Go to a quiet place and ask yourself, "Am I fully surrendered to God?" If the answer is no, ask the Holy Spirit to show you what areas of your life still need to be submitted to Him. There is more that the Lord wants to do in and through your life — so much more! Trust Him and be quick to obey what He tells you to do.

NOTES

Mike Signorelli. *From Chaos to Clarity: No Turning Back*. Self-published, Amazon, 2022.

TOPIC

Behind the Seen

SYNOPSIS

Dr. Frederick Price approaches the Scriptures with careful study and uses his vast knowledge of the Bible to communicate wisely about the times we're living in. In today's lesson, he teaches from his book *Behind the Seen* and addresses hot-button issues, including fallen angels, the Nephilim, portals, UFOs, and aliens. He expresses that we don't have to fear what's in the unseen realm, but we do need to understand it in order to be effective in these last days.

As Fred and the "sons of Issachar" discuss what is happening "behind the seen," you will discover answers to questions you might not have realized you had — questions like, What happens when you pray? How is technology affecting society today? What fearful sights are we going to see at the end of the age? Can Christians be "abducted"? You won't want to miss this!

The emphasis of this lesson:

The hidden agenda of the unseen realm is being revealed in our society more every day, but as believers, we know where our help comes from. Although the enemy would like to intimidate and scare us, the truth is, we were born for such a time as this, and the power of God is with us wherever we go. As you learn more about what is going on behind the seen realm, you will be empowered to stand up to darkness and expose the plan of the enemy. Jesus is the Son of the living God, and just as He promised in Matthew 16:18, the gates of hell will not prevail against His Church!

There Is More Than Meets the Eye

As we saw in the last lesson, there is a lot of chaos in the world around us, but have you ever wondered whether there was someone operating behind the scenes, stirring up the chaos and confusion that seem so prevalent today? It's easy to blame other people for the devastating things we see on the news or the anger and frustration we face in our own cities and nations day after day, but what if there was something more at work?

The Bible tells us in Ephesians 6:12 that we wrestle not against "flesh and blood." As tempting as it is to blame other people, our battle is a *spiritual* one against powers in an unseen realm. And when we understand how it works, when we understand spiritual laws and principles, then we are better equipped and prepared to handle what we do see in the physical or seen realm.

One clear example of the unseen realm affecting what happens in the seen realm is found in Daniel 10. Daniel had been praying over an issue for quite some time, and then one day, an angel suddenly appeared to him. The messenger told Daniel, "The moment you spoke those words, Heaven heard, and I was dispatched to you, but the Prince of Persia withstood me for 21 days" (v. 12-13). The angel had been dispatched to Daniel the moment he began praying, but he was delayed by the prince of Persia, a principality of the kingdom of darkness. Heaven heard Daniel praying, but who else heard him? The kingdom of darkness — and it dispatched its own agents to contend with the agents of God. Daniel's prayers released God's angelic messengers to go to work, but they also alerted the forces of darkness to oppose and thwart the plan of God.

Just like Daniel, the moment you declare the Word of God in prayer, God hears it and *immediately* dispatches emissaries to work on your behalf. You might not realize it, but as a child of God, your words carry great authority and power. That means that sometimes when you pray and wonder, *Is my prayer ever going to be answered?* It may not be that you're doing anything wrong; it could be that powers of darkness have been alerted and are attempting to thwart the plan of God for your life. This biblical example reveals that when you are aware of the forces of Heaven and hell that are at work behind the seen realm, you will have greater wisdom and understanding in how to address what is happening in the seen realm.

Be Careful *What* and *How* You Hear

As believers we can become so accustomed to the environment around us that we begin to copy what the world says instead of obeying and believing what God says. One reason this happens is because we are not careful about what we hear and listen to.

In the program, Mike Signorelli said, "I've been feeling a really strong pull to just warn the Body of Christ about their input, because what happens is, from the abundance of the heart the mouth speaks. So if you're constantly taking in this Babylonian agenda, Babylonian lyrics — which really is demonic — then what'll happen is sometimes there will be this mixture like salt and freshwater coming out of the same spring."

It is very important that we do not become so familiar with the brokenness in the world around us — ingesting all the same media, movies, and music — that we pollute the spring of our soul. We must be vigilant to renew our minds with the Word of God and guard what we take in through our eyes and ears so that our mind, will, and emotions will remain strong.

Jesus said in Mark 4:24, "…Take heed *what* ye hear…," and He also said be careful *how* you hear (*see* Luke 8:18). Sometimes what we hear in the media or other people say is just wrong. But other times, we can hear something incorrectly, so we need to be careful what we hear as well as *how* we hear what is being said to us.

Fred elaborated on this and said: "The *what* is the content, and the *how* is the intent." Sometimes what a person says isn't offensive, but someone takes offense to it because of *how* they heard it. Other times, a person may say something that is just wrong and flat out offensive. In that case, *what* they said was wrong. It's not only important that we watch what we say, we also need to keep watch over how we hear or perceive what someone else says to us.

Will the Nephilim Return?

Because Fred addresses the subject of fallen angels and Nephilim in his book, Alan DiDio posed the question to Fred, "Will there be a resurgence of the Nephilim, and if so, what is that going to look like?"

Fred responded that while he doesn't believe Nephilim will appear as they did before the Flood, he does believe we'll see aberrations, anomalies, and hybridizations which were prevalent in the days of Noah and the Flood. In fact, there are many examples of these hybridizations already on the earth today.

At the time Nephilim roamed the earth, many people and creatures transgressed boundaries that were never meant to be crossed, and there is an important difference between a *transgression* and *sin*. In the program, Rick said, "Did you know, in the Greek world, the word 'sin' was nonexistent? They did not have an understanding of sin. The word for 'sin,' *hamartia*, means *a mistake*. It could be intentional or it could be accidental — it was a flaw. But the word 'transgression' means *to intentionally violate a boundary or a barrier*.

"What happened in the world before the Flood? The world before the Flood was the day of 'trans' — hybrid creatures, fallen angels that broke barriers, that intentionally did what they were not supposed to do, trans creatures. And what's the big word today? It's trans. It's the end of the age, as it was in the days of Noah. Here we are again. People are transgressing boundaries and people are trying to change their gender. Laboratories across the world where they're not monitored are trying to break all kinds of boundaries and create things that should never be created. We're living in the day of trans. And just like Fred said, we may not see actual giants, but we're going to see all kinds of hybrid aberrations during our time."

The "sons of Issachar" were largely in agreement that while there may not be a resurgence of physical giants like the Nephilim, we will continue to see aberrations and abnormal creatures emerge as the boundaries of our natural world are transgressed.

We Are Living in a Day of Lawlessness

As lawlessness increases and the boundaries of our physical world are violated, or transgressed, more and more, it will open access points from the unseen realm to the seen realm. The nefarious activity of crossing boundaries that were never meant to be crossed is providing access where it was never meant to be given. And this is not just a contemporary problem. We see evidence of this in the Bible as well.

When King Saul wanted an answer from the Lord and did not receive it, he sought out the witch of Endor, and by means we're not sure of, Samuel, who was dead, appeared (*see* 1 Samuel 28:6-15). There are many differing opinions among scholars as to whether or not it was Samuel that Saul saw and talked to, and a few opinions are shared in the program, but the point of this biblical example is that when people seek to violate a boundary God has made and cross it, it can open a portal to the unseen realm.

As humans we are gatekeepers to the supernatural. Whether or not we're aware of it, believers and unbelievers alike are free moral agents who dictate what can happen between the spirit realm and the natural realm (or the unseen and the seen). And this is not something we should take lightly.

One interesting subject that is discussed in the program is the Large Hadron Collider (LHC) built by the European Organization for Nuclear Research (CERN). This group does not disclose all the projects they are working on, so there is some mystery here, but one major concern among people is that they will use this machine to try and communicate with the unseen world. Essentially, people are worried this machine could open portals to the unseen realm and wreak havoc on our world. If this is indeed the case, it could be similar to what occurred at the Tower of Babel.

Aliens, UFOs, and 'Fearful Sights'

In his book, Fred also touches on the subject of aliens and UFOs, and in the program, he said that First Corinthians 15:40 tells us there are two bodies. One is terrestrial and the other is celestial. We as humans have terrestrial bodies while we live on the earth, and heavenly creatures, like angels, have celestial bodies. He offered this statement: "I don't believe that there are other terrestrial alien creatures. In other words, creatures that may live on another planet.... I believe that the aliens people have encountered are celestial creatures."

One interesting example that applies to this discussion is found in Ezekiel 1:15-17. Ezekiel had a vision in which he saw four cherubim and beside them four ophanim, or four wheels. These wheels could move in any direction without turning, as verse 17 says "they turned not when they went." When people have described the movement of UFOs, which move like no aircraft can move, it sounds just like the movement of these celestial creatures, the ophanim, described in Ezekiel 1.

You might be wondering, *Since when did people become so interested in aliens, UFOs, portals, and Nephilim? What does this have to do with me?* In Luke 21, Jesus warned us that when we see wars, rumors of wars, pestilence, famine, etc., taking place, they are signs that we have arrived at the end of the age, and in verse 11, He added that we will also see "fearful sights and great signs" from the heavens. This means that celestial activity and monstrous, hybrid creatures are not only real, but they are also expected to appear in these last days.

While talking about these subjects may be unsettling to some, remember that we do not have to be afraid. Jesus told us these things, not to scare us, but to prepare us. He has the wisdom, power, protection, and answers we need for the days ahead because He has already overcome the world (*see* John 16:33). So don't give in to worry or fear; come to Jesus and ask Him for what you need.

Know Who You're Fighting For

So how should the Church respond to our society's growing obsession with Nephilim, seeing things come out of the heavens, or building monstrous things? Our answer is *Jesus*.

In Matthew 16, Jesus asked His disciples, "Who do men say I am?" Then He asked them, "But who do you say that I am?" Peter responded, "…Thou art the Christ, the Son of the living God" (v. 16). What was true then is still true now — *Jesus is the Christ and the Son of the living God* — and the reality of this claim is meant to shake our world.

Fred posed this thought to the other "sons of Issachar" in the program: "Just imagine if everyone in the Body of Christ answered that question boldly and loudly, *'Who do you say that I am?'* and we started telling people who He is, who He really is." What do you think would happen? If the Body of Christ rose up and boldly declared who Christ really is to people, it would heal hearts, draw them to Him, and expel the kingdom of darkness like never before. Simply declaring the truth of who Jesus is, is powerful!

But that's not all. Jesus went on to say in verse 18 "upon this rock" He would build His Church and the gates of hell will not prevail against it. That was a bold claim, and Jesus made it for a good reason. Fred explained: "I believe that was Jesus picking a fight. I believe He was being aggressive, and I believe He was being on the offensive. And I believe that is what believers need to be doing today. Not just waiting to be attacked but being on the attack."

It is important to note that, again, we are not attacking other people. We're fighting against the powers of darkness in the unseen realm who are manipulating behavior in the seen realm. While we are definitely called to stand up for truth and the principles God has given us to live by in Scripture, we are never called to be hateful or derogatory toward others for any reason.

What About Alien Encounters?

In the program, Joseph Z shared that his wife Heather had an encounter with a celestial being of some kind, but instead of giving into fear, she took authority over it in the name of Jesus and it vanished. While there are some documented accounts of people who claim to have been "abducted" by aliens, not one has been reported by a Spirit-filled Christian who knows his or her identity in Christ. What does that tell you? "Aliens" don't like the name of Jesus, and when you take authority over them in Jesus' name, *they take off running!*

Fred confirmed this in the program, saying: "You'll know if it's benevolent or malevolent by that name." When you say the name of Jesus, it is going to expose that entity for what it is. And remember, we have no reason to be scared. James 2:19 tells us that when we use the name of Jesus, demons *tremble.*

Rick said, "Do you know what that word 'tremble' means? It means *to be spooked or panicked.* When you say the name of Jesus, you *spook* them. Whether it's a demon or anything else you're looking at, if it's from an evil source, that thing will take off running. You can panic it and spook it just by the mention of Jesus' name."

You do not have to fear anything or anyone on this earth. Just speak the name of Jesus the moment you feel anything evil has invaded your space, and you'll spook it so badly it will leave you.

How To Pull Down Strongholds

Remember, our words have *power*, and the weapons of our warfare are so *mighty* they can pull down strongholds (*see* 2 Corinthians 10:3). So how do we pull down strongholds? We find the answer in Romans chapter 10.

Romans 10:6 (*NKJV*) says, "But the righteousness of faith speaks in this way...." This tells us there is a manner in which the righteous speak. When you have a stronghold, you need to be careful how you speak. You shouldn't be speaking words of negativity, worry, or doubt. You need to speak faith-filled words confidently and boldly as you declare who God is and put your complete trust in Him.

As you speak those words of faith and daily live out the principles in God's Word — praying and interceding, worshiping, living a lifestyle of holiness — His words will become your words, and that strongholds will start to crumble until it's completely gone.

Alan made this statement: "Consistent discipline and faithfulness to the Word of God is the key to deliverance in this last hour." And that is the truth. There is a way you need to speak, but you also need to commit yourself to daily walking in obedience to the Lord and His Word. As both work together in harmony, you will see every stronghold in your life disappear.

STUDY QUESTIONS

Study to shew thyself approved unto God, a workman that needeth not to be ashamed, rightly dividing the word of truth.
— 2 Timothy 2:15

1. What is the difference between a *transgression* and *sin*? How does this relate to the Nephilim and the nefarious activity we are seeing in the world today?

2. What heavenly creature is described in Ezekiel 1? Is this something you have heard of before? What other celestial creatures are mentioned throughout the Bible?

3. James 2:19 says demons *tremble* at the name of Jesus. Read Philippians 2:10. What else does the Bible tell us happens in response to the name of Jesus?

PRACTICAL APPLICATION

But be ye doers of the word, and not hearers only, deceiving your own selves.
— James 1:22

1. Fred says in the program that the battles we face in life are spiritual ones, not against flesh and blood. Have there been any instances in your life in which you found yourself fighting against another person versus the spiritual influence behind the *seen*? In what way was that successful or not? Describe your experience.

2. In this lesson, we discussed the power of saying out loud who Jesus is. Take a moment to say out loud the truth of who Jesus is to you and what He has done in your life. Sing it, shout it, exclaim it! He

deserves all the glory! As you do this, notice how your environment changes.

3. Do you have any strongholds in your life? Reread the last section of this lesson. What are two things you can do every day to begin tearing down that stronghold? Write them down and commit to do them each day until that stronghold is gone.

NOTES

Frederick K. Price, Jr. *Behind the Seen: Angels, Demons, and the Battle for the Human Soul.* Los Angeles, CA: Lightly Salted Publishing, 2019.

LESSON 5

TOPIC

Summoning the Demon

SYNOPSIS

In this lesson, Alan DiDio shares shocking insights from his book *Summoning the Demon.* He speaks authoritatively and decisively about new technologies that are emerging, unearthing the truth about artificial intelligence and the effect it is having (and will continue to have) on society as a result. With research and documentation to back up his claims, Alan exposes the agenda of the enemy and those cooperating with him and encourages the Church to take a stand while it still can.

Discussing topics from alien abductions and AI interfacing to drone technology and the mark of the beast, the "sons of Issachar" cover a lot of territory and ask bold questions. As they share studied opinions on these interesting topics, they again emphasize the importance for believers to know the authority they have in Christ and to study the Word of God so they are prepared for the last days ahead.

The emphasis of this lesson:

The Bible has a lot to say about the issues we're facing in these last days. That means we don't need to be shocked, surprised, or impressed by the

crazy events and developments we're seeing take center stage. Instead of being afraid, we need to understand our authority in Christ as believers, open our eyes to what is happening in our world, and tell people the truth about what the Bible says regarding these things.

Alan DiDio shared that he was inspired to begin studying artificial intelligence (AI), and eventually to write his book *Summoning the Demon*, after watching an interview with Elon Musk in which he warned people that AI will never be something we can control. In an effort to provide a balanced, objective study to the Body of Christ, Alan approached the research from a skeptic's point of view and was surprised by what he found. Although he covers much more in his book, these are the main points the "sons of Issachar" discussed.

Is This a Biblical Apocalyptic Moment?

Although we have been discussing the realities of the times we're living in at length throughout these lessons, let's take a look at how those who are not Christians are perceiving what is happening in the world. According to recent reports, about 42 percent of Americans believe that Jesus could return in their lifetime. What makes that number shocking is that there are not even that many people in America who claim to be Christians. Another fascinating survey recorded that 14 percent of agnostics and 9 percent of atheists said they believe they are living in the end times, meaning they believe they are living in *a biblical apocalyptic moment*.

People are looking at the world around them, the news, and the media, and they recognize that something unusual is taking place. Even atheists are recognizing there is a dark force that is pure evil. There is a general understanding across America, and likely around the world, among the religious and non-religious that these are dark days and could be the last days.

Now what does that mean for you? That means people's hearts are more ripe than ever to be ministered to with the Gospel of Jesus Christ. In the program, Alan said, "The end times is probably the greatest apologetic we have at our disposal to win people to Jesus."

The word "apologetic" means to give a defense or an answer for what we believe, and in this context of sharing the Gospel, Alan meant that we have the greatest opportunity to give people an answer for the hope that lies within us. Vast portions of the population in the U.S. know they are living in the last days and realize they're not ready for it, but as believers, we understand the times we're living in and can share the everlasting hope we've found in Jesus with those who don't yet know Him.

Alan made this comment: "Maybe religion and politics is difficult to talk about at Thanksgiving dinner or at Christmas, but everybody loves talking about aliens, Skinwalker Ranch, and Project Blue Book. These are all fun things, but we have a more interesting narrative as Christians about these things. It's just that the world has been lying well, and we [the Church] have been telling the truth badly."

While certain topics of conversation may not have been open for discussion in the past, the undeniable events that are taking place today have grabbed people's attention and have led them to think seriously about whether or not they are living in the end times. Whether you are offering a critic a biblical perspective or encouraging someone who is lost and looking for hope, you have the answers they need. Now is not the time to stay silent; it is the time to understand for yourself what the Bible has to say about the end times and share that truth with those you meet.

Aliens and Alien Religions

Christians have so marginalized the subjects of aliens and UFOs that they laugh at anyone who talks about them. But this is a mistake. These subjects are live issues that have dominated our culture and are affecting our society every day.

Alan made this comment on the program: "You have senators and congressmen who actually buy into an alien religion. Mormonism is an alien religion. They believe their god lives on a planet called Kolob and that he has many spirit children, and if you are a good Mormon, you can have your own planet too.

"Then you have people like Tom Cruz who are credited with saving Hollywood. He believes Scientology is an alien religion. John Travolta, too.... He believes in an alien religion. Not only that: the largest alien religion in the world is atheism. Richard Dawkins, the author of *The God Delusion*, said that he doesn't believe God exists or that God created the world but that life on earth could have been seeded by aliens."

A lot of people either believe in these alien religions or think that life could have been seeded by aliens. And the more high-profile government officials and celebrities that claim to do so, the more we will see this dominate our culture. We can't pretend this is a fringe issue anymore; it is already a prevalent issue in society, and if the Church does not rise up and give a biblical answer for what is true, Alan proposes that aliens will likely be part of the great end-time deception.

Project Blue Book

In Alan's book *Summoning the Demon*, he does a deep dive into previously classified documents from the U.S. government associated with Project Blue Book. For context, Project Blue Book was an initiative to carefully investigate sightings of unidentified flying objects (UFOs) that were being reported across the country. Although this may seem like a far-reaching claim, many documents that have been recently declassified from this project are confirming the validity of such sightings.

Alan showed a copy of one such document on the program that was recently declassified, and it's also photocopied in his book. It was a memo from September 23, 1947, which reported a legitimate phenomenon occurred. Essentially, it described the movement, shape, and appearance of the flying object and confirmed that what was observed was not fictitious or made up.

Again, this is not a fringe issue. There are many documents that have been concealed for decades that are just now coming out, and there have even been congressional hearings about these things. It is important for believers to have an understanding of this subject.

A Full Disclosure

Joel Renner asked an important question in the program. He said, "Alan, why would you say that this has been concealed? Why are they, or why is the government, concealing all this information?"

Alan supposed that the reason these documents are coming out and there are congressional hearings being held is because new laws have been enacted to protect people who come forward with this type of information. Now when people provide this information they can't be politically persecuted or fired from their job.

Rick added that he believes the powers that be are preparing the world for a full disclosure. They're letting pieces of information come out, but soon they'll make a big announcement. And if believers are not sure what the Bible says about this subject, their faith could be shaken by it.

This is not something to take lightly, but we also don't need to be scared. Each of these things is addressed in the Bible, and as we've seen in these lessons, if we know what Jesus said concerning them, then we won't be scared or impressed by what the world says about them.

The Truth About Artificial Intelligence

In Revelation 13, the Bible tells us the antichrist system will be controlled by one man who can dictate who buys and who sells. We have never known how that would be possible before now, but with AI, it is now possible for a small number of people to control the world economy from one small room, dictating where and when people buy and sell.

The development of AI has even been described by many as something that could upend civilization. In fact, 48 percent of 4,000 AI researchers were surveyed, and 48 percent of them said they believe there's a 10 percent chance AI could upend civilization. So there is great risk involved in this, but we are still barreling toward it as fast as we possibly can because the potential for technological advancement is so great.

You might be wondering, *What is AI and how does it work?* Artificial intelligence essentially describes computer learning or computers being able to learn, process, and distribute information, but there is a spectrum of AI and how it operates. On one end, you might think of Terminator 2 or SkyNet, but AI also includes search engines like Google and automated phone messages, like when you call your credit card company and hear a recorded voice direct you through prompts. So in this way, AI has been around for a long time.

Google was actually developed as an AI company who wanted to create a god-like mind. All these years of operating as a search engine allowed the technology to learn and understand human personality. It has been collecting that information for years and years in order to learn human behavior. Social media is another example of AI. As you use it, it begins to suggest new things that you might like and want to look at or new profiles that might interest you. All of those algorithms and automations are examples of AI, a computer learning and adapting to what you do and how you use it.

In the program, Alan presented the possibility that the way AI will dominate society and upend civilization may not be by booting up robots with guns to subdue and destroy things. It may be through the subtle manipulation and suggestive use of things like social media that gradually dictate and change our human behavior. In fact, there is evidence that it is already happening now. He said, "I think we will impute consciousness to it [AI] long before it's conscious in an effort to be a more tolerant society that people love."

The 'Technology Singularity'

Joseph Z asked Alan to elaborate on what he calls the "technological singularity." Alan said a "singularity" is what happens within a black hole. Once you enter it, all the known laws of physics break down and you can't predict what's going to happen. So the "technological singularity" with AI is the moment we cross the line technologically where we can no longer predict what's going to happen with it, namely because we've never had anything like it before. When we cross that line, we will have reached the technological singularity, which is a dangerous place to be. Alan said, "This is not an invention. It is the creation of an inventor that is going to be able to revolutionize society."

People have likened AI to what it would be like for an other-worldly entity to visit the earth. We wouldn't know when the creature would come, but we'd know it was going to arrive at some point and it would be better than us at everything. If that was the case, we would take some time to prepare for that interaction and not rush into it blindly. That is what AI is like. We are on the verge of creating these systems that are smarter than us and better than us at everything, and we're not slowing down to prepare for the moment that line is crossed.

How Should We Respond?

So what does this mean for the Church? And knowing that AI poses many risks, how should we respond? Alan made this powerful statement in the program: "Artificial intelligence is simply the enemy's attempt to replicate the gifts of the Holy Spirit. Everything that AI promises to do, the gifts of the Holy Spirit have been doing for 2,000 years. From healing to deliverance, to wisdom, to guidance — we just need to lean on the gifts and the grace of the Holy Ghost."

Be encouraged! We are overcomers as children of God, and the Bible tells us greater is He that is in us than he that is in the world! (*See* 1 John 4:4.) The enemy is just a copycat, and he is doing his best to replicate what God has already given us. But there are also practical things you can do. **First**, choose not to be afraid. **Second**, understand your authority in Jesus Christ. **Third**, get involved with AI now and be as influential as you can.

Alan explained that by using AI we are showing it how we want it to operate; essentially, we are training it. And if you are concerned whether you will be participating with the spirit of the antichrist by using AI, you are not. AI is just a tool the same way a gun is a tool. We want to utilize the weapons we have, so we need to be involved with AI while we still can.

Rick gave the example of when the first televisions were invented. Back then many Pentecostals didn't want to use it because they believed TVs were part of the antichrist system, but they missed an opportunity. The same thing later happened with computers too. Technology is a tool, and the way it is used depends on who is controlling it.

How Far Is Too Far?

Joel mentioned that there is technology developed by a company called Neuralink that allows them to implant brain-computer interface chips into someone's head. There are two people who are currently walking around with these devices in their heads. Alan responded that we should definitely avoid any technology that asks us to forfeit our will. Anything that interrupts your ability to choose freely is extremely dangerous.

Technology implanted into humans this way is called transhumanism. And many of the "sons of Issachar" agreed that this is one way the Nephilim activity is occurring in our world today. It is crossing a boundary of technology and human biology that was never meant to be crossed, creating a trans, Nephilim-like hybrid.

Another troubling example that was mentioned in the program is new technology that allows you to pay for items by scanning your palm. And there are even European countries that don't require passports; instead, they have a machine that scans your face. The Bible is clear the mark of the beast will be a mark on the forehead or right hand of people, and each of these technological developments seem incrementally normalizing this behavior to eventually lead in that direction.

Project Blue Beam

Todd Coconato asked Alan whether a fake alien invasion may be part of the great end-time deception that is coming. Alan wrote on this in his book but briefly, Project Blue Beam was a theory posited by a Canadian journalist who said that the powerful elites would eventually use technology to create a messianic-type moment in the skies. It is highly possible this would be done using drones, similar to one of the recent Spider-man movies.

Project Blue Beam said two things would happen. First, there would be some sort of natural disaster that uncovers archaeological evidence disproving the Bible and showing that all religions need to come together. Second, there would be another cataclysmic event in the skies created by technology that would make people think it was an Armageddon-like event or a second-coming event that would cause people to stray away from Christianity and buy into the enemy's lies.

If this type of event does happen, it does not mean we need to change our theology or even be surprised that it does occur. Jesus has already told us in Luke 21:11 that there will be "fearful sights and great signs" from the heavens. And there is nothing the enemy can throw at us that Jesus has not prepared us for. Remember, greater is He that is in you than he who is in the world!

STUDY QUESTIONS

Study to shew thyself approved unto God, a workman that needeth not to be ashamed, rightly dividing the word of truth.
— 2 Timothy 2:15

1. We have discussed aliens and UFOs in two lessons so far. What have you learned about them that you didn't know before? Why are these subjects important to understand as believers?
2. Two examples of alien religions were mentioned in this lesson. What were they?

3. What is a "technological singularity," and why is it important to consider in regard to artificial intelligence? What risks does this pose for our society?

4. Alan made the statement that AI is the enemy's attempt at recreating the gifts of the Holy Spirit. What are the gifts of the Holy Spirit? Where do we see them listed in the Bible?

PRACTICAL APPLICATION

**But be ye doers of the word, and not hearers only,
deceiving your own selves.**
—James 1:22

1. Just as Alan said in this program, the days we are living in provide a great opportunity to share the Gospel with the lost. Are there people in your life who have been closed off to hearing about the Gospel? Would any of the topics in this lesson serve as an entry point to you sharing the Good News with them? Take a moment to pray and ask the Holy Spirit to open a door you can use to share the love of Christ with them.

2. Have you had any fear surrounding the use of AI or the topics of aliens and UFOs? What could you do to educate yourself on these topics more and remind yourself what the Bible has to say about them?

3. First John 4:4 says God is and will always be greater than the enemy and anything he plots or comes up with. Do you believe that statement? Why or why not? What can you do to encourage your faith and remember the truth of this verse?

NOTES

Alan DiDio. *Summoning the Demon: AI, Aliens, and the Antichrist*. Shippensburg, PA: Destiny Image Publishers, 2024.

TOPIC
Built Different

SYNOPSIS

In this lesson, Gabe Poirot takes the lead to reveal several lessons he has learned while sharing the love of God with young adults and teenagers from his generation, teaching them to pursue the Lord wholeheartedly. After growing a social media following of 2,000,000 on YouTube and nearly 2,000,000 on TikTok, Gabe wrote his book *Built Different* to encourage people to walk in the security of who they really are in Christ. As he shares from his heart, Gabe reminds us that Jesus runs after the lost and expects us to do the same, no matter how uncomfortable or unfamiliar it may feel at first.

Covering topics like depression and anxiety, gender confusion, and what it's like to grow up without a father, this new group of "sons of Issachar" illuminates even more ways the Church can take an active role in this late hour. While so many young people seem to be misunderstood and confused, there is a great opportunity to bring them into the family of God. And this lesson will show you how!

The emphasis of this lesson:

If you, or someone you know, have struggled to know your identity in Christ, it is time for you to receive the spirit of adoption from your heavenly Father. You were made in the image of the living God, and as you gaze at His face, you will begin to see who you really are. Don't be afraid to step out into the beautiful plan He has made for you because you were made for such a time as this.

Gabe Poirot is a joyful follower of God with a heart to reach his generation. While he originally wrote his book *Built Different* for teenagers and young adults who are often referred to as "Gen Z," or Generation Z, this devotional also holds powerful truths that apply to any generation, regardless of age. There are many in society that struggle with depression, anxiety, and mental health, but even more there is a huge number of people who struggle to know their identity. God laid this book on Gabe's heart to reach those who are hurting and who don't know their identity in Christ so that they can find true healing and family in Him.

As we take a closer look at Gabe's story and some of the realities this younger generation is facing in culture today, you will be encouraged to embrace even more deeply who you are in Christ as well as how you can run toward those who are hurting and show them the love of Christ.

Gabe's Personal Testimony

After he wrote his book, Gabe had an unexpected accident. In the program, he shares the following:

> I was on an electric skateboard without a helmet of course, and I fell off the skateboard while I was racing a car, cracked my skull in half, and instantly was in a coma for the next two and a half weeks. I was not supposed to live.
>
> The hospital asked for my last will. They called my parents in from Virginia, and they talked about me in past tense, asking everyone what I was like. And I was lying there on the hospital bed, death bed really, with my skull cracked in half, and my lung had failed. I was breathing once every 60 seconds. They were going to drill into my throat because I wasn't able to breathe anymore, but then, the week of November 12, the Spirit of the Lord brought me back and showed mercy on my life.
>
> When you say, 'How did that happen? How did I come back?' That's a longer message, but it's the agreement of God's Word in synchrony with His sons and daughters on the earth that gives Him the ability to answer prayers. There were many, many people praying for me....
>
> When you get that close to the veil of life and death, you finally start to understand the difference between truth versus everything that is presented to us here on this earth. And I'll tell you, Rick, 99.9 percent of everything we ever go through down on this earth is such a plastic, false reality compared to Truth Himself.

Gabe shared that an experience like that where you come so close to the veil of life and death leads you to finally understand the difference between truth versus everything that is presented to us here on this earth.

Coming that close to Jesus, encountering Love Himself, makes you realize He is more real than you could ever understand.

Hope for Gen Z

So how do we share the reality of Jesus and His love with this upcoming generation? We need to first understand the struggles they are facing.

Gabe reported that 30 percent of people in Generation Z don't know their gender, or in other words, one third of young adults don't know their identity. That means in a stadium filled with 100,000 people from 14 to 25 years old, 30,000 would come forward saying they don't know who they are right now. They are being indoctrinated by culture and the media to question who they are, and when they come home, there is no one there to tell them anything different.

The majority of people in this generation lack a strong father and mother family unit. In many places, roughly 60 to 70 percent of kids don't have a father and mother who are married before they were born, and in some areas, it's upwards of 90 percent. Often the father isn't even in the home regardless of whether the parents are married. He's completely absent.

While these statistics are staggering, there is still hope. Gabe said, "This is what is on the surface, but I'm telling you, Rick, there is revival in Generation Z and there is great hope for not just this generation, but also Gen Alpha, which is upcoming, and really for everyone on this earth. There is great hope.

"Because of everything that has come against us, we're becoming like a boomerang, and we're saying, 'Not today!' There's a rising group of both young and old that are done with the sickos. We're done being manipulated, and…they're going to take back the land. We've reached that place so there is great hope."

Despite the fact that we see the repercussions of identity confusion in this largely fatherless generation, there is still great hope rising as many from Gen Z are beginning to speak out and stand for truth.

A Crisis of Fatherlessness

This issue of fathers being absent from the home is one that many people have experienced. Philip Renner shared that as he preaches on the streets, people become completely undone when the subject of fatherhood is mentioned. It is a wounded place for many, whether their father abused them or was just completely absent.

But even fathers in the home can be absent. They may provide for the family and protect the family, but they don't take up their mantel to be the priest and prophet of their home. They don't lead their family to the Lord or speak the truth of God's Word to their wife and kids, so there is still this absence that makes a big hole even if they're present physically.

The Bible tells us the enemy comes only to steal, kill, and destroy (see John 10:10), and that is what we're seeing. The enemy has come against this younger generation and has been attacking God's Word and attacking their identity in Christ. Psalm 139:14 says we are fearfully and wonderfully made and Ephesians 2:10 states that we are His workmanship, created in Christ Jesus to do good works that He prepared for us beforehand, but this generation has been sold the lie that they should question who they are and what gender they are. They are more lost and confused than ever, not knowing who they are in Christ, let alone which bathroom to use.

Gabe made this helpful observation in the program: "It's easy to get into judgment where we say, 'How could a person ever not know who they are? Why are they so against God? Why is this next generation so off?' But what I've found time and time again is this next generation isn't knowingly going on this path. It's out of their pain and their hurt."

This is so important to understand. You have more than likely had your own experience with teenagers or young adults from Generation Z, and maybe the way they looked or dressed or spoke was offensive, off-putting, or at least difficult for you to understand. But remember, they are people who are hurting, and they need the love of Christ. Instead of getting into a critical place or a place of judgment, open your heart in compassion and let the love of Jesus flow out of you to them.

How To Recover Identity

So how do we respond to this pandemic of fatherlessness? Romans 12:2 (*NKJV*) says, "And do not be conformed to this world, but be transformed by the renewing of your mind...." Just as we saw in earlier lessons, what we listen to and allow into our mind matters. It shapes how we think and what we believe about ourselves — it even begins to shape our identity. So it is vitally important that we carefully choose which voices we listen to.

As Ben Diaz said in the program, we're always renewing our mind to something. Many people today, both young and old, spend exorbitant amounts of time on social media, and this can have a detrimental effect. When someone spends hours online scrolling and watching videos compared to the short amount of time he reads his Bible, his mind is going to be out of balance, and it will be difficult to counteract the lies and nonsense that he listened to. But it doesn't matter what the distraction is — social media, movies, music, games — if we are not drawing near to our heavenly Father to hear what He has to say more than we are listening to entertainment from the world, we are going to get off track and forget who we are.

Philip made a powerful statement in the program. He said: "The identity is in the sperm, it's not in the egg, and the father carries the sperm. So when you take away the father, which is what has happened to this whole generation, you lose identity." Fathers are the ones who speak identity over children. And while single mothers do an incredible job raising children on their own, it is still the father who is meant to speak identity over them.

Regardless of what your experience has been with your own earthly father, when you received salvation, you received the Spirit of adoption from your heavenly Father (*see* Romans 8:15). And when you understand this is your reality as a child of God, you will know what it's like to have a perfect Father. You will experience the fullness of His love that makes you secure and causes you to know who you are.

What Should Fathers Do?

Although there is a lot of pain that can come from a father being absent, there is an even greater opportunity for healing and recovering of identity when a father fully steps into the role God has given him.

Even if a father has to travel for his business or must work long hours during the day, he can choose to be fully present with his family while he is at home. This may not be what feels easy or most convenient, but this is the unique role God has given to fathers. And even when time is limited, the time a father spends being present and intentional with his children will minister to their souls.

Gabe gave this encouragement to fathers in the program: "No matter where someone is watching this TV program from, it's important that we all have a secret place where we seek the Father on our own. And for every father, the best thing you can do is look at the face of your heavenly Father. Because the more you look into His face, you will see yourself through the mirror of His eyes. And as we see Him, we will see ourselves in Him, and we will reflect Him wherever we go."

Every single one of us — mother, father, grandmother, grandfather — need to have our own secret place to retreat to and seek the face of our heavenly Father. We are the only creatures God made in His own image. He made us fathers and mothers, and when we go back to understanding our identity through the eyes of our heavenly Father, we will fit into the puzzle that He made just for us and our life will make sense again. We need to hear firsthand who our Father says we are and get back to the plan Christ made for us to walk in from the start.

The Church Needs To Respond

Joel Renner asked Gabe, "What do you think is the answer for this identity crisis in this generation?" And Gabe responded that instead of preaching at a teenager or someone in the next generation, it is important to first listen to them. If we want them to listen to what we have to say, we need to first show them we care about them, be present in their life, and sow into that relationship.

These young men and women may look much different than you, but the truth is, those with a wild appearance are often crying out for help. And to reach them with the love of Christ, it's going to take us not being afraid. Instead, we are called to run right to a person like that and become their friend, start conversations with them, and invite them into life with us because otherwise they will find an alternative.

This type of evangelism is what we have mentioned in several previous lessons, and truthfully, it should be natural for us all as believers and followers of Christ. The issues we're facing in our culture are not going away quietly. We need to stand up to the darkness, show people we are not afraid of them, and fervently show them the compassionate love of Christ.

If we will sacrifice our lives and what we think we want and, instead, give in to what the Lord has for us, we will see the world change. It is that simple. Thirty percent of this younger generation does not know who they are, so we need to do our best to bring correction and rescue the perishing. Jesus is merciful, Jesus will save, and Jesus wants us to reach this generation.

STUDY QUESTIONS

**Study to shew thyself approved unto God, a workman that
needeth not to be ashamed, rightly dividing the word of truth.
— 2 Timothy 2:15**

1. What do Psalm 139:14 and Ephesians 2:10 say about your identity? Do you believe you are "fearfully and wonderfully made"? What "good works" do you think God has prepared for you to walk in? Write out your answers.

2. How many teenagers and young adults question their gender according to the figure Gabe mentioned in this lesson? What do the "sons of Issachar" believe the reason is for this widespread identity crisis?

3. Why is it important for us to watch what we see and listen to? According to Romans 12:2, how does this affect our thinking?

4. In the program, Gabe said that when we go back to understanding our identity through the eyes of our heavenly Father, we will fit into the puzzle He made just for us and our life will make sense again. What puzzle did God make for you? Read the following scriptures and reflect on what specific purpose God has called you to fulfill:

    • Second Timothy 1:9; First Peter 2:9; Ephesians 4:1-3; John 15:16

PRACTICAL APPLICATION

**But be ye doers of the word, and not hearers only,
deceiving your own selves.
— James 1:22**

1. Have you had a difficult relationship with your earthly father? If so, read Romans 8:15 and ask the Holy Spirit to give you a deeper understanding of the Spirit of adoption you've received. Practice coming to that place every day until you receive a revelation of the love your perfect heavenly Father has for you.

2. If you are a father, what are two things you can do to be more intentional with your children? Write them down and set a time to do them this week.

3. In the program, Gabe talked about how important it is for every believer to have a secret place where they meet with the Lord. Do you have a place like this where you retreat to pray? If not, brainstorm

three different quiet places where you can spend some uninterrupted time with God.

NOTES

Gabe Poirot. *Built Different: 90 Days to Becoming all God Wants You to Be*. Shippensburg, PA: Harrison House Publishers, 2022.

LESSON 7

TOPIC

A Fasted Life

SYNOPSIS

Philip Renner leads a ministry dedicated to *shocking the darkness*, and that is something we definitely need in the times in which we're living. Although the world is growing darker and darker, the Church is called to grow brighter and brighter. As Philip shares from his book *A Fasted Life*, you will learn firsthand what it looks like to live a life of intimacy and power with God.

Philip and his team go to some of the darkest places in the U.S. to share the love of Christ, and as he shares personal testimonies of what God is doing in those places, you will be inspired to give your heart wholly to Jesus and pursue the lost around you too. You do not want to miss this "sons of Issachar" discussion as the group, again, reveals what God will do when believers take a stand for His name and His Word and boldly love the lost in these last days.

The emphasis of this lesson:

Experiencing the power of God is as simple as hearing His voice and doing what He tells you to do. Although doing what God asks can seem scary, Philip reminds us that we are surrounded by a shield of favor and we have what other people need — the love of Christ. Don't be afraid to love the people that God has asked you to love. He is with you, and He will give you wisdom to know what to do.

Philip Renner wrote his book *A Fasted Life* not just about fasting, but also about living a life of hearing God's voice and doing what He tells us to do. The culture we're living in is growing darker, so to navigate the end-time storms ahead, we need to be led by the Spirit of God. That is what Philip will teach you to do in his book and in this lesson.

Shocking the Darkness

Throughout Philip's ministry, the Lord has revealed to him the power worship has to shift the atmosphere of a city when believers lift up their hands and praise Him. But more recently, the Lord took him deeper. He told Philip to take authority and "shock the darkness." He asked Philip to go to places where the darkness would be absolutely shocked that he showed up, meaning places that believers almost never go to because they are either too scared or they've just been taught not to go there. Places like the largest gay parade in America, cities in the U.S. where you could be stabbed or shot, and events where there is debauchery of every kind.

Most recently, Philip and his team went to the largest gay parade in the U.S., which took place in Washington D.C. There were 600,000 people at this parade, and 973 people got saved. Philip said that when his team began to worship, people just started walking up to them with tears running down their faces. A lot of them had grown up in church, and they recognized the songs he and his team played. This is because many in the gay community used to go to church and believe in Jesus. In fact, one statistic says as much as 70 percent of the gay community are backslidden Christians, and often this occurs around the age of 18 when most people go to college.

Philip and his team have also been to several areas where people are often stabbed or shot. One such place that they ministered in was Kensington, PA, one of the most drug-infested cities in America, and they went to a part of the city called "Zombieland" where 300 to 400 bodies of people line the street, decaying and covered in blood. As Philip's team drove through the streets, people took rocks and started throwing them at their cars. His team wanted to leave, but Philip knew they needed to stay and love on those people, so they parked the cars and went out to meet them.

Philip made this powerful observation: "One of the things that we've been indoctrinated to think is if somebody looks scary, if somebody looks different, then they're too far gone. And what we said in the other program was that it's a cry for help.... You feel like your flesh is saying, 'Get out of here. This is dangerous. They're going to steal my guitar; they're going to steal my coat; they're going to steal everything, sell it, and buy more drugs.' But when you understand that they're in pain, and you talk to them with love, with compassion, and you see them for who they really are — which is made in the image of Christ — it doesn't matter if it's a gay parade or it's Kensington. The result is the same. We walk up to them, we sing a blessing over them...and tears are just going down their eyes. And there's a word of knowledge about their past or about sickness or disease or something that is going on, and they're completely undone. They say, 'I need this Jesus.'"

On another trip, Philip went to San Francisco, CA, and they saw several injection stations set up near the City Hall. The government had lined up all these drug addicts at stations to give them clean needles. They weren't trying to provide an answer to their problems; their solution was to give them clean needles so they could continue harming their bodies. That just shows us the futility of man when he does not have the answer of the Gospel.

You Have a Part To Play

It is easy to hear about these stories and think that these are issues only impacting a fringe part of society, but that is a lie. There are devastating things happening in every city across the U.S.

Philip said, "I just dare you to go online and look at 'events in my city.' And it'll scare you the amount of satanic events that are taking place, the gay events that are taking place, and all the different concerts that have a ton of agenda, where people come back from those concerts and they kill themselves. There is a reason for every single church to be having a prayer meeting every single night because the devil, he is consistent. He's after the next generation because he knows that if he can change the mindset of one generation, then their kids are going to grow up differently and believe the same thing."

While you may not have a whole team with you to go to each of these places where Philip and his team have gone, there is still something you can do. You can always pray — and remember prayer is *powerful* in activating the unseen realm. You can also learn from Philip's example and participate in this Kingdom work by shocking the darkness with your presence and loving the people in your city who might seem hard or scary to love.

Burning Man

Another large event that Philip attended with his team was Burning Man, a week-long event held in the desert of Nevada where 80,000 people come and completely let themselves go, participating in fornication and debauchery of every kind. It is known for the huge, wooden structure of a man that is burned on the last day.

Philip said that 20 percent of the people there were completely naked and another 20 percent wore nothing but a type of mesh fabric. They walk around naked and do drugs, have sex — do all kinds of things — and this is not just a bunch of hippies in the desert. These are billionaires, politicians, music stars, entertainers, and the globally elite who attend — in Philip's words, half of Silicon Valley is there.

The reason people come to this event is because the giant structure of a man is a ziggurat. It's like a spiritual tower where all these people from various religions all over the world come together — shamans, witch doctors, and warlocks — and do their satanic acts. It's not just a place of sex and drugs; it's a place where you can be a part of almost every single religion in the world. It's similar to how the Bible describes the spiritual activities of Babylon. Everyone was extremely open spiritually, and while their nefarious activities didn't reach the heavens physically, they did reach the heavens spiritually. That is what Burning Man is.

So Philip arrived with his team at Burning Man, yet another place where they knew they would almost certainly be kicked out, and they decided to set up right in front of the cops. But Philip knew that he and his team were covered by *a shield of favor* from the Lord (*see* Psalm 5:12), and you are too. No matter where you are — at school, at university, in the workplace, in the world — there is a shield of favor around you, covering you wherever you go.

The first person who got saved at Burning Man was the stepdaughter of one of the men who founded it 36 years before. Philip was so encouraged seeing that God was in what they were doing, so he took his team and went right to the Burning Man structure.

The Burning Man is an idol, a massive effigy of a man, where people at the event throw all their past, anxiety, and depression so that at the end it will burn with the man. Philip and his team stood right at the base of the structure and began singing blessings over people. As they sang, people started crying, saying they didn't expect to see that. They listened and knew it was real, so they said, "I need more of Jesus," and Philip and his team shared the Gospel with them. And this wasn't groups of two or three people; these were groups of 15 or 20 people at a time.

Philip said, "Then it got so easy. I was like, 'Lord, you are in this.'" He took his team and climbed the stairs of the base of the Burning Man statue so they could look out over the whole area. From there they gave an open-air altar call and continued singing blessings over people.

Amazingly, Philip heard one of the Burning Man watchers, who are like the security guards at the event, say to another watcher, "I wish I could kick them out, but I don't have the authority." And hearing that was prophetic because leading up to the event, Philip had quoted Joshua 2:11 hundreds and hundreds of times, which says they are terrified of us because the Lord has given us the land. From there, the Lord just kept doing miracle after miracle.

How Do We Respond?

We are living at the end of the age, in the last of the last days, and we can either wring our hands, saying, "Oh, it's so terrible, it's so bad that the world is getting darker," or we can get bold in the Spirit. The answer is not to sit in our house and close the shades. We are completely equipped with the power of the Gospel to go to these people who are confused, to rescue the perishing, and to care for the dying.

In the program, Philip gave some guidance in how to do this. He said the way to reach these people is not with a blow horn, preaching at them without building any kind of relationship. It's not through being judgmental, calling people names. It's through truly caring about them and showing them the love of God.

Love Is Not Inclusivity

Philip shared a story about interacting with an "inclusive" church, which is not really a church, while he and his team were at the gay parade in Washington D.C. This is what happened:

We sang over them and preached the Gospel and then one of the leaders or elders of that church walked up to me and said, 'Hey, can I take the microphone and tell them to clean up after the gay parade?' And I said, 'Well, I don't think there's anything that bad about that.' But…they took the microphone and said, 'We just want to thank our queer god for queerly creating us.' That is literally what they said. So we took the microphone, and we said, 'First of all, God is not queer. He didn't queerly create us. We are made in His image — male and female. You can't live however you want to live. You have to live a life of holiness, and we love you guys.' And if there was ever a place where I thought a riot was going to take place, it was during the gay parade.

Although it caused a stir, what Philip did was love those people and tell them the truth. That is what God's shield of favor and love enable us to do. It helps us look at people through God's eyes. We are not called to be critical of people, call them names, shout at them, or judge the way they look. They've already been kicked out of churches; they've already been called names. Instead, talk to them and love them. At the end of the day, the Bible says that he who has no sin can throw the first stone (see John 8:1-11).

How To Love a Child Who Has Gone Astray

Joel Renner said, "I can just hear someone at home right now saying, 'My child has gone astray.' Philip, what would you say to that parent?"

Philip's encouragement to any parent who has watched his or her child go astray is first not to judge them but love them. Love is the most powerful force on the planet because God is love, and you can speak the truth in love without judging somebody. That is something the Church really needs to learn. Second, pray that the Father's love is revealed to them. This younger generation has experienced the absence of their earthly father, and they need to be adopted by Abba Father and experience His love.

Rick added this helpful clarification: "The problem is not judging — judging is just a part of life. It's being judgmental that is an issue. Being judgmental doesn't help anybody; it doesn't change anybody to be judgmental of him or her. To judge that something is wrong is okay, and you can judge something is wrong without being judgmental of that person. But being judgmental is just being condemning and being ugly. It's not helpful."

At the end of the day, we need to believe the best and call out the best in our children. Remind them who they really are. And we also need to pray for laborers to be sent across their paths. Once children reach a certain age, it's important for them to have their own walk with the Lord, so praying for solid, godly friends and mentors in their life is crucial.

STUDY QUESTIONS

Study to shew thyself approved unto God, a workman that needeth not to be ashamed, rightly dividing the word of truth.
— 2 Timothy 2:15

1. What examples of "shocking the darkness" do we see in Scripture? Read First Kings 18:20-40. What do you notice about Elijah in this story? Are there any similarities between Elijah's challenge and Philip's ministry?

2. According to the statistic recorded in this lesson, what percentage of the gay community used to be in church before moving into that lifestyle? At what age does this seem to occur most often and why?

3. What is one thing Philip says you can do to see what events are taking place in your city? Take a moment to do it and reflect on what you find.

PRACTICAL APPLICATION

But be ye doers of the word, and not hearers only, deceiving your own selves.
— James 1:22

1. One of the observations Philip made as a result of his ministry is that most people are in pain and hurting and once you treat them with compassion and see them for who they truly are, they are receptive to the Gospel. Who is someone in your life that has been difficult to love? What is one way you can show the love of Jesus this week?

2. Do you have a child or relative who is currently living a gay lifestyle? How successful have you been at speaking the truth in love versus being judgmental or critical of them? If you need to, repent and then ask the Holy Spirit to lead you in how to love them well. The Holy Spirit is our Teacher and He knows the key to every heart (*see* Psalm 44:21).

3. Do you believe a shield of favor surrounds you wherever you go? No matter what environment you face, God will protect you and surround you with His love. Read Psalm 5 and reflect on what it says.

NOTES

Philip Renner. *A Fasted Life — Living a Lifestyle of Intimacy and Power With God.* Shippensburg, PA: Harrison House Publishers, 2021.

LESSON 8

TOPIC

Does God Still Heal Today?

SYNOPSIS

In this lesson, Ryan Edberg opens his book *Does God Still Heal Today?* to reveal that it is God's desire and will to heal 100 percent of the time. Despite the bad teaching you might have heard regarding healing, God does not need to make up His mind about whether or not to heal you. He already bought that healing at the Cross, and He's ready to give it to you freely!

As the "sons of Issachar" gather in this program, they discuss many misconceptions about healing and share testimony after testimony of times when God miraculously healed them and people they've ministered to. There are more medicated and hurting people in America than ever today, but the good news is, Jesus gave us authority to lay our hands on the sick and pray for their healing. Get ready to have your faith stirred as these powerful ministers of God share the truth about healing.

The emphasis of this lesson:

We don't have to beg or convince God to heal us. We simply need to take Him at His Word and freely receive what Jesus already paid for. If you are ready to see breakthrough in your life and the lives of others, begin laying your hands on the sick and praying in faith and watch what God will do!

Ryan Edberg has traveled with Joseph Z doing ministry for 25 years, and as part of that ministry, he has preached at several youth conferences. Over time he noticed people were confused about what the Bible has to say about healing, so he wrote his book *Does God Still Heal Today?* At events where he has taught on healing, he has seen countless people healed simply because they got their bad thinking and bad theology about healing out of their head. God is the giver of every good and perfect gift, and one of those gifts is *healing*. We'll take a closer look at that in this lesson.

Healing Is a Finished Work

There is no doubt we are living in the last days, and although the world around us is growing darker, the Church is going to rise up in a bigger way. There are going to be signs, wonders, and miracles that happen, and if you want to see those results in your own life, you need to do it the way the Bible says to do it.

A lot of people believe God is the Healer, but when they need healing, they beg and plead with Him to heal them as if He is going to say yes or no. But healing was paid for in full at the Cross along with our salvation. Isaiah 53:5 says, "…With his stripes we are healed," and this tells us the beating and scourging Jesus bore as His blood was shed for you and me totally and completely purchased our healing.

When you are saved, you don't go to Jesus and say, "I believe in You now and I want to be saved, so please go die on the Cross for me." Instead, you receive something that was already paid for. You take your faith and attach it to what Jesus has already done on the Cross. It is the same for healing. Instead of begging God to do something, you can do exactly what He told you to do in the Bible and receive your healing and breakthrough today.

You Don't Need To Get God's Attention

In the program, Rick said, "You know, a lot of people think that God responds to tears, that when you cry and when you're sincere — God does not respond to tears. God responds to faith. Now you may cry as you express your faith, but if all you give God is your tears, you've not done anything to move God. It is your faith that moves God."

The Bible tells us that the Pharisees would tear their clothes and put ashes on themselves to try and get God's attention, but the truth is, we already have God's attention (*see* Psalm 33:18). Notice Isaiah 53:5 says by His stripes we are *healed*, past tense. So we can rest assured, this is a finished work Jesus has already accomplished and we don't need to get His attention to make sure we get it. We simply need to come into agreement with what He's already done.

And this is the same for any biblical principle. When we fast, we are not doing it to get God's attention. We do it because we love Him. And when we worship, we're not trying to impress God or get something from Him. We do it because we adore Him and He is worthy of our praise. Healing is not something God is withholding until we close our eyes and pray just right. He is a good Father, and He has made this gift freely available to us.

It's Hard To Argue With a Miracle

One type of critic Ryan often faces when he teaches on healing is cessationists. We've mentioned cessationism in a previous lesson, but as a reminder, cessationists are those who believe the gifts of the Spirit ceased when the last of the 12 apostles died. When someone who believes this way encounters Ryan's teaching on healing, he'll say, "I don't believe like that. You can't teach like that." But the miracles that occur in these conferences and meetings are proof enough. What God's Word says about healing is true.

Rick shared in the program that he understands where these people were coming from because when he was younger, he grew up in a church that did not believe in healing or the gifts of the Spirit. Then one day his aunt took him to a Kathryn Kuhlman meeting that blew his mind, and he saw people getting up out of wheelchairs. And it was hard to argue with that!

Ryan said, "One miracle can answer a lot of arguments," meaning that while people seem to have plenty to say when they disagreed with what he preached, but when they encountered a healing miracle for themselves, they were at a loss for words. Ryan shared that instead of arguing with people, often he'll ask them, "Can I just pray for you?" And then when God heals them, there's no debate anymore.

God Has Given You a Guarantee

People want to be touched by God and experience His healing, so why does it seem so hard at times to receive? One thing that you need to understand is it is always God's will to heal. If we could convince God to heal us, then our healing would be based on works, not faith. But God is our Father, and He loves us. We don't need to convince Him of anything. He already cares for us more than we know (*see* 1 Peter 5:7).

First John 5:14 and 15 says, "…If we ask any thing according to his will, he heareth us: and if we know that he hears us, whatsoever we ask, we know that we have the petitions that we desired of him." God's mind is made up — it's not a matter of *maybe God will heal me* or *if God wills it, He will heal me*. It *is* the will of God to heal you, and you need to resolve that question in your mind.

Now, there may be things that block us from receiving that healing, like disobedience, sin, or unbelief, but it is always God's will to heal. If we will line ourselves up with the will of God and ask Him for healing according to His will, we will have the petitions we have asked of Him. That is a scriptural guarantee!

Ryan gave this example: "If I bought a brand-new car and it was sitting in the driveway, you wouldn't have to wonder if I want to drive that car. I want to drive that car because I paid for the car. It's the same thing with healing. We don't have to question if it's God's will for us to be healed. If He paid for it, He wants to use it."

The Bible is clear about God's will to heal, and we can trust that because God isn't a confusing person. He doesn't play games with us or lead us to question what He says. Everywhere throughout the Bible, every chapter and every verse, He makes it clear to us that He always wants the best for us.

Lay Your Hands on the Sick and They Will Recover

Rick shared the following testimony in the program:

> Just last week, Denise and I were in a hotel, and when I came in the morning, I saw the hostess and she could hardly walk. She was in so much pain. She had a bulging disc. I mean, she was limping, she was crying.
>
> I said, 'Are you alright?' She said, 'No, I'm not alright. I've been to the emergency room four times in the last 48 hours. I have to go to work because I need to earn money. I cried all night for God to heal me." I prayed for her and then Denise came in. And Denise is really bold when it comes to healing.

Denise looked at her and said, 'Sweetheart, I am going to pray for you.' Denise prayed for her then said, 'Alright, now do what you couldn't do. Let's go walking.' She began walking and immediately felt better. And Denise said, 'You just keep it up.'

Well, when I got up early the next morning, I came downstairs to get a cup of coffee, and the other hostess said, 'Where is your wife?' I said, 'She'll be here soon.' And the hostess said, 'She needs to get here. She needs to hear what happened to the other hostess! She slept all night. She's dancing, she's rejoicing, she's completely healed!' I mean that woman was dancing all over that restaurant, really healed.

Healing ministry is needed right now more than ever before. In the U.S., for instance, people are overmedicated and overfed, they don't eat right, and they don't exercise. People everywhere are sick and taking some sort of medication. And we are not against medication — we are for medication if you need medication — but as believers, we need to know the healing power that is in our hands.

The laying on of hands is listed in Hebrews 6 right in the middle of the six major doctrines of our faith, which means using our hands is very important. Throughout Scripture, we see that Jesus healed with His hands, and in Mark 16:18, Jesus told us to lay hands on the sick and they'd recover. This is because healing virtue flows through our hands, and if we get our hands out of our pockets and start laying them on people, the percentages of people that get healed would be greater. We might not see every person healed, but if we'll start laying our hands on the sick and praying, we'll see the percentages of people who receive their healing manifestation go up and up.

Gabe added this: "We have nothing to lose! Everyone always questions whether or not they should pray for someone else, and I think, *Well, their situation couldn't get worse, so why not pray? Why not lay hands on the sick and see them recover?* I remember there was a Muslim boy in my high school who was deaf, and I was about to not invite him to our Bible study because I was thinking that would be a crazy miracle to see him healed. And the Lord convicted me, saying, 'Gabe, that is little for me.' And we invited him. Sure enough, the Lord opened his ears, and he gave his life to Christ the next day."

There's no reason for you to be afraid of praying for someone else's healing. But if you're concerned that nothing will happen or that there won't be an instantaneous miracle when you pray, look at First Corinthians 12:9 and 10. It lists both the gift of healing and the gift of miracles, showing us they are two different things. A miracle is instantaneous, but the word "healing" used here describes something that happens over a period of time. It is the Greek word *iaomai*, the word for *a doctor*.

When you go to the doctor, you don't expect to be instantly healed, but you do expect to leave with the goods that will help you begin to recover. That is what the word *iaomai* describes, and it is the same word used in Mark 16:18, which says when we lay hands on the sick they will recover. So the next time you pray for the sick, if you don't have the faith to believe for them to be instantly healed, lay hands on them and pray that they will receive the goods they need to recover and begin reversing their condition. And from that moment forward, they are going to get better.

There's More Than One Way To Heal

Often with healing, we can ask God for wisdom in what foods to add into or take out of our diet or what lifestyle changes to make that will empower our bodies to heal and stay healthy. Philip shared this personal testimony of a time the Lord healed him:

> I remember when the doctor told me, 'You'll never sing again, and you'll croak like a frog for the rest of your life because of the nodules.' And I remember I left that place, and the Lord gave me Zephaniah 3:17. He said, 'Even if you can't sing, I'm singing and dancing over you.'

> For the next year, I did change foods. I changed the way I slept. I even changed the way I sang — I sang lower, I didn't always sing high. But I remember I was quoting the Word of God over and over and over again. And it looked like things just got worse and worse until one day I got completely healed when Billy Burke prayed for me, and I watched those nodules fly out of my mouth like marbles. And now I can sing better than I ever sang before.

> But here's the interesting thing, my mindset has also changed. I sleep more than I did. I eat different than I did. I don't drink stuff that's full of sugar. I don't do stuff that would hurt my vocal

cords. But that's the result of the healing because it was not only a healing of my body, it was also a healing of my mindset.

A lot of people get healed in their body, but because they don't change their mindset, they go back to the same patterns and routine and get sick again. They might even get worse than before. This is because we have free will. But despite the challenging environment or circumstances, God's will is still to heal.

Ryan shared these two testimonies in the program:

> I was preaching at a school with 500 students in a denominational setting. They were cessationists.... Long story short, I just taught on the will of God and how to find your calling in life. This girl came up to me, and she was bawling because she couldn't find the will of God in her life. Because God's will was that she played professional volleyball one day, and she had hurt her back. I said, 'I don't know if that's the will of God for your life, but I do know that He's the Healer. Can I pray for you?' I prayed for her back, and I said, 'How do you feel?' And she said, 'Exactly the same,' so I said, 'Well, we'll be believing,' and just kind of moved her on.

> At lunch she came up and just started moving and bending and moving all around. She was totally healed, but it didn't look like a lot to me because she was just bending and moving.... But at the end of the event, they asked what testimonies had happened — and this was a place that did not believe in that — and this girl got up there and said, 'I just want you to know my back...' and then she started moving and the whole place just started to yell, so I knew this was something different.

> The kids started to yell, scream, and they all made a line. I started to pray for kids, and God was touching every single kid, healing them. My faith before was like, 'I'll be believing for you,' and now it was like, 'Bring out your dead!' Because God was touching everybody.

> This one girl who helped us was deaf in her ear, and she came up, but she didn't want prayer for healing. I said, 'Why? I thought you couldn't hear.' She said, 'It's not my hearing. My dad hit me in the head when I was a kid with a pipe. It's in my brain.'

I said, 'It doesn't matter if it's your ear or your brain. God is the Healer. He created you, so it's not a big deal to Him. When I pray in your ear, you just stop me when you can hear.' And I said, 'In the name of Jesus,' and she stopped me and said, 'I can hear.'

But she said it in a weird way. Everybody else was freaking out and losing their mind, sobbing and just worshiping God, and she said, 'I can hear,' and walked off. I thought, *If Jesus prayed for somebody twice, I can pray for somebody twice.* So I went to find her.

She was on the phone. I came up behind her, and I heard her say, 'No, Mom. This *is* my deaf ear. I'm talking to you out of my deaf ear,' and she was just sobbing. It really spoke to me because I was looking for a reaction; I was looking for goosebumps; I was looking for something, and God was just looking for His Word.

When God heals, it might look different every time. It's not our job to find a formula that says if we do A, God will do B. God is simply looking for His Word to come out of our mouth wrapped in our faith. We don't need to say just the right prayer or hold our hands just right. We simply need to declare what the Word of God says, believe it, and ask for His healing to come.

One common mistake people often make when praying for the sick is not asking them to do something they couldn't do before. In the gospels, when Jesus healed the sick, the word that was used the majority of the time to describe it is the Greek word *therapeo*, which is where we get the word "therapy." Jesus didn't just lay hands on the sick, He told them to do something they couldn't do before — "Pick up your bed," "Walk," "Stretch out your hand," etc. But many times when we pray, we leave before asking people to do anything. The next time you pray for the sick, ask them to do something they couldn't do before because it's when they stretch forth their hand that the manifestation of their healing comes.

You Are Needed in These Last Days!

People are hurting and broken everywhere you go, and they need the healing power in your hands more than ever before. Joseph Z made this powerful observation about the times we're living in: "I believe that the reason the gifts of the Spirit have been fought so hard and the reason that the power gifts and the declaration or the demonstration of the Spirit has been fought so hard is because it's the most vital weaponry we have going into the last days."

The spiritual gifts we have been given are under attack, but this is a spiritual battle, not a battle against flesh and blood. People are in need more than ever, so we can't hide our spiritual gifts away. We need to use them to bless others just like Jesus told us to. And remember, one of the most powerful things we can do is simply live out the Gospel with our actions. Whether that means praying for the sick, giving a word of knowledge, or simply being kind to someone, when you use your unique gifts, you are presenting people with the Gospel and love of Christ.

STUDY QUESTIONS

Study to shew thyself approved unto God, a workman that
needeth not to be ashamed, rightly dividing the word of truth.
— 2 Timothy 2:15

1. Why isn't healing something that we need to earn or beg God for? What evidence did the "sons of Issachar" give for this?
2. Ryan taught that we don't need to get God's attention in order to be healed. Why is that true? What was wrong with how the Pharisees tried to get attention from God?
3. We discussed God's will to heal a lot in this program. Why is knowing what God's will is concerning healing important when we read First John 5:14 and 15?
4. What is one common mistake people make when praying for the sick? Think about how often the Greek word *therapeo* was used to describe how Jesus healed.

PRACTICAL APPLICATION

But be ye doers of the word, and not hearers only,
deceiving your own selves.
— James 1:22

1. Have you ever experienced the healing power of God in your life, whether that was instantaneous healing or healing that took place over a period of time? Share your experience and reflect on what you learned through that time.

2. Hebrews 6 mentions the biblical doctrine of the laying on of hands. Have you ever laid hands on someone and prayed for them? What was your experience? How do you think you'd approach a similar situation now after reading this lesson?

3. Who are the people in your life right now that need to receive healing? Take a moment to pray for them, and if you're able, go to them and lay hands on them and believe they will receive what they need to recover.

NOTES

Ryan Edberg. *Does God Still Heal Today?*. Self-published, Amazon, 2023.

LESSON 9

TOPIC

Supernatural Healing of the Soul

SYNOPSIS

In this powerful lesson, Ben Diaz shares from his book *Supernatural Healing of the Soul* and reveals how to demolish wrong thinking at the root so that it doesn't have any power over your life. Pulling examples from his own life, he explains the difference between being healed and being made whole and even gives instruction on how to tear down strongholds brick by brick from your mind.

With input from each of the "sons of Issachar," the discussion touches many pertinent topics, like why many Christians pray but never see breakthrough in their life, how to weigh every thought by the Word of God, why it is so important to forgive, and so much more. This is a program you do not want to miss!

The emphasis of this lesson:

There is an epidemic of confusion in our society, but that is not how God wants you to live. He wants to address the root issues in your heart so that you can truly live free. There is no emotional, mental, or physical

wound too deep or too severe for His healing touch, and as you commit yourself to do what the Bible says, you will find that your soul can be not only healed, but made whole.

The Lord gave Ben Diaz a revelation of Jeremiah 1:10 (*AMP*) a few years ago, which says: "See, I have appointed you this day over the nations and over the kingdoms, to uproot and break down, to destroy and to overthrow, to build and to plant." Ben noticed that four out of those six words of instruction are about demolition. It led him to think about how often Christians focus on building and planting but never do the demolition work. He wrote his book *Supernatural Healing of the Soul* to help people become whole by demolishing wrong thinking and attitudes from their lives.

In the last lesson, we looked at physical healing, and in this lesson, we'll focus on the healing of the soul — the mind, will, and emotions.

Get Down To the Heart

What goes on in your head affects your whole life. Your mind acts like a huge filter that everything is sifted through. But interestingly, you form the majority of your opinions and worldview very early in life. Most children form 80 percent of their belief system by the age of eight years old, and statistics show that most adults do not waver from these beliefs very much.

In society, we often see people gravitate toward various forms of behavior modification to change habits they don't like, such as new diets, new workout programs, new devotionals, etc. But these kinds of activities simply manage the symptoms of a deeper problem. They don't usually get down to the heart and address what's really going on.

One of the most common symptoms we see is that people are confused. They have anxiety or depression, they are on medication, their family is broken up, their children are struggling, and they don't know which church to go to. Some people don't even know whether or not they should be going to church at all. People are in a state of mental and emotional confusion, and that is why receiving healing of the soul is so important.

Proverbs 4:23 (*NIV*) says, "Above all else, guard your heart, for everything you do flows from it." This tells us that all good and bad things in our lives flow out of our heart. In this way, our heart is like soil — whatever we plant in it is going to produce fruit.

People are always planting seeds in their heart whether they realize it or not. Just like we are always renewing our mind to something, our heart is always producing fruit from the seeds we plant in it — and *majority rules*. This means whatever we plant the most will expand and occupy our heart and mind. In other words, what we empower and focus our attention on will be magnified. That's why the Bible tells us to magnify the Lord (*see* Psalm 34:3). When we magnify the Lord, He becomes the biggest thing in our life, and all our problems and worries shrink away in comparison.

The Obstacle of Bad Teaching

Sometimes believers can get frustrated because they pray and pray and still don't see the promises of God manifest in their life. Have you ever encountered this yourself? It might even be made more difficult by new believers, younger in their faith, coming to your church asking God for the same thing, and instead of having to wait, they suddenly see crazy miracles happen right away. You might be wondering, *Does the Lord love them more?* But the answer is, no, of course not! They simply may not have as much opposition built up in their belief system that is working against the Word of God.

Look at the example of the Parable of the Sower in Matthew 13. Some seed fell on good ground and produced 30-, 60-, or 100-fold, and some seed didn't produce anything at all. The seed that didn't produce anything was drowned out by different things. This could include our belief system, our self, or our subconscious that believes something wrong that is working against the Word of God.

As Joseph Z says, "The only thing that's worse than no teaching is bad teaching." When someone has been in religion receiving bad teaching for many years, there can be a lot of un-teaching, or demolition, that is needed before a breakthrough can occur.

Uproot Bad Thinking

So how do you demolish wrong thinking in your life? First, take every thought captive. This doesn't mean just bad thoughts — take *every* thought captive, good or bad. Ask yourself, "Does this line up with the Word of God?" And if it doesn't, throw it out. If it does, hang on to it. You'll know it lines up with God's Word if the thought lines up with is whatever is just, whatever is pure, whatever is holy, and whatever is of good report (*see* Philippians 4:8). Second, you can tear down strongholds in your mind, brick by brick if you have to.

Usually if you have wrong thoughts in your mind, they don't come down all at once. It takes tenacity to remove them. You have to face those thoughts and say, "I'm going to pull that down even if it takes me every day of my life. I am committed to work at this, and I won't be finished until I have disassembled, dismantled, and eradicated my mind and heart of this issue."

Rick shared this story in the program: "When I was a boy, my dad wanted to build a garage, and we didn't have a lot of money but we needed a lot of bricks. So my dad purchased an old, dilapidated house in downtown Tulsa, and every day he'd put me in the truck and we'd go downtown with our hammers. And one brick at a time, we began to dismantle that house. I thought it would take forever because once we knocked one brick out of the wall, we had to knock all the old mortar off of it. Then we'd put it in a clean stack and go for the next brick and the next brick. But brick by brick, we took that thing down to the foundation."

That is the same commitment you need to have to become free. You need to decide you will dismantle those wrong thoughts until there is nothing left. Then when you're down to the foundation, you can begin to build the right thoughts.

What Is a Stronghold?

In order to help us better understand what kind of things we are dismantling, Ben gave this definition for what a stronghold is: "I say that a stronghold is an accumulation of thoughts over years compiled with false evidence."

Strongholds begin with the devil throwing the seed of a lie into your heart or mind. That lie could be anything. For example, maybe you grew up in a home where your dad is rude to your mom. The seed that is planted after watching that behavior could be: All men are evil. And over time, the devil continues to build, brick by brick, upon the foundation of that lie. He begins to point out any evidence he can find of men being evil or men being out to get you until you start looking for that evidence yourself. Then after years of compiling thoughts on top of that lie, you've built a stronghold, and it's cemented with the false evidence you've gathered and witnessed for years. And suddenly, when someone says something that is the truth, like not all men are evil, it is much harder for you to believe and agree with that truth because there is an entire stronghold working against it.

Strongholds are like towers that you build in your mind. Think of the tower Rapunzel is trapped in in the fairy tale. It seemed very safe at the top of that tower, but she wasn't free. She was trapped, and that can be how it feels when you have a stronghold of your own working against the truth of the Word of God. You might be trying to believe for a promise in Scripture to happen in your life, but if you have a stronghold you've spent most of your life building that is working against it, it won't happen.

Back to our example, if a girl who has a stronghold built on the lie that all men are evil decides to get married, she could end up sabotaging her whole marriage because of that stronghold. It would cause her to be on high alert and have a suspicious spirit, constantly analyzing everything her husband does, and that would create a lot of turmoil in that relationship. But there is hope! While it can take decades to build strongholds, by the grace of God it can take a fraction of the time to tear it down because He is helping us do it.

How To Destroy a Stronghold

So what is the first step in tearing down a stronghold? First, you need to identify what the stronghold is. Ask yourself, "What lie am I believing?" And if you're not sure, ask the Holy Spirit to guide you. He is the One that leads us into all truth (*see* John 16:13), and we need His direction to know what is at the root of our wrong thinking.

Once you have identified the stronghold, you need to start replacing those lies with the truth in God's Word. Second Corinthians 10:5 says, "Casting down imaginations, and every high thing that exalteth itself against the knowledge of God, and bringing into captivity every thought to the obedience of Christ." From this we know that a lie is anything that is contrary to what the Bible says, and the second half of the verse tells us what to do with those lies, "bringing into captivity every thought to the obedience of Christ."

Take hold of each thought one by one, dismantling that stronghold brick by brick, and ask whether or not it lines up with what the Bible says. This can seem like a tedious process, but it goes a lot faster with the Holy Spirit leading and helping you. It doesn't have to take years to do. You can tear down a stronghold in a matter of months, but it will require you to be diligent and to meditate on the Word of God so you can renew your mind.

So if the Bible says you are healed, but the devil says, "You're sick. You're always going to be sick," *that is a lie* against what God says about you. And if the Bible says you are righteous, but you walk around feeling condemned all the time because the devil is telling you, "You're never going to get free of this," *that is a lie.* It goes against what the Word of God says about you.

In this process of dismantling a stronghold, you need to open your ears to the right thing (God's Word) and close your ears to the wrong thing (the lies the devil has thrown at you). There will always be two voices speaking to you, but you need to determine which voice you will listen to because the one you listen to is going to dominate you.

You Can Fight Back

Philip Renner shared something that has helped him, and that is not just quoting a scripture but worshiping with that scripture. He went on to say this: "And when I go into that place of the presence of God, that's where God does the impossible. That's when He touches me. You know, there's a scripture that is often quoted in the Christian world, Luke 10:19, which talks about believers being given authority to step on scorpions and snakes…but not many people know verse 20. What verse 20 says is: 'Don't rejoice that the demons listen to you and you can cast them out, but that your name is written in the Book of Life,' which means there can be no demonstration of the power of God, there can be no transformation, without first spending time in His presence."

Often believers get excited to see the power of God at work in their lives and the lives of others, but they don't take the time to first meet with Him and draw near in His presence. There is a real battle going on for your mind, so if you want to be free of the strongholds in your life, it is vital that you spend time in the Lord's presence every day. It's in that place of intimacy with Him that true transformation can happen.

In Romans 7:23, the apostle Paul wrote that there was a law in his members warring against the law of his mind. He was describing what we've been talking about in this lesson. There is a battle, a war, going on for your mind, and the mind is like an incubator because what you focus on and think about you will begin to create. If you've created stronghold after stronghold in your life, it's time for you to ask, "What am I thinking about?" and then start fighting those thoughts with words. You can't fight thoughts with thoughts; you fight thoughts with *words*. As Rick often says, "Sometimes you need to stop thinking and start speaking to yourself."

Your voice is your authority, and you need to use it. If all you ever do is listen to your mind, your mind will run you all over the place. But part of the demolition process of tearing down strongholds is using your voice, speaking to those thoughts, and telling yourself what you need to think.

It's Time To Tell Your Thoughts Where To Go

In Second Corinthians 10:5, the phrase "taking every thought captive" actually describes *the point of a Roman spear*. The point of Roman spears were so sharp that if a soldier put it into the back of a captive or rebellious person, he could point them in any direction he wanted them to go. And when our mind is speaking to us and running us all over the place, it's time for us to use our voice and point our voice like a spear into the back of those thoughts, saying, "No, I'm going to direct you. You're not going to tell me what to feel. You're not going to tell me where to go. You're going to obey me."

David also shows us an example of this in the book of Psalms. He said, "Bless the Lord, O my soul; and all that is within me, bless his holy name. Bless the Lord, O my soul, and forget not all his benefits" (Psalm 103:1,2). He didn't wait for his soul to get on board. He told his soul what to do.

Both the devil and God are territorial. They both want your mind. The devil knows your heart belongs to Jesus, so he's not after your heart; he's after your mind. And what you look at and dwell on really matters. Over time those images and thoughts will cement those strongholds in place.

Your Thoughts Are Not Your Identity

It is proven scientifically that we have the ability to step outside our thoughts and look at them, which tells us we are not our thoughts. Sometimes people get so entangled in their thoughts that they think they are their thoughts. In fact, that is what happens when people feel condemned. They begin attaching the thoughts they're having about themselves to their identity. But the truth is, most of the bad thoughts come from the devil. That's what he does — he plants false evidence and then he accuses you of having them.

The devil throws all these bad thoughts at you, then you assume those thoughts are your own, and you start attaching them to your identity. But it started as a seed, one thought that grows in your mind, and you start to replicate that lie or that thought with your own thoughts. You might begin thinking, *I'm a pervert. I'm a dishonest person,* because he's accusing you of those things.

The enemy is the most jealous creature, and he accuses us of that which he is guilty of. It's exactly what he did with Adam and Eve. He was so jealous of them because he wanted to be made in the image of God, he wanted to be God himself, so he tempted Eve to be her own god.

The Power of Forgiveness

Joel Renner shared this powerful thought: "A lot of thoughts can be demolished, or start to be demolished, by forgiving. I think it's like if you have a tower of bricks, you can pull that bottom brick out and the rest will crumble if you forgive. People who put that first thought in your mind, if you forgive that person, it can take down a lot of walls."

This is a key part of the process in tearing down strongholds and bad thoughts from your mind. When we pray for a stronghold to be demolished, we're not starting at the top of the tower. The Holy Spirit goes right to the bottom because He knows if you take out the root, the rest of that tower will crumble. Often removing that bottom brick in a stronghold requires forgiveness.

Healing vs. Wholeness

Jesus didn't just pay for us to be healed; He paid for us to be *whole*. Healing has to do with the physical symptoms, but wholeness has to do with becoming whole *inside* your heart and mind. It addresses your foundation, your belief system, the things that were broken in childhood or through trauma. And the good news is, once those soul issues are addressed, you are equipped to sustain healing.

Healing on its own is not enough. Many people receive healing but lose it because they can't sustain it. God will heal us every time we ask Him to, but it takes a deeper, inner healing to not only change the way we eat, for example, but also the way we think about our body. And it's the same with prosperity. We might be stuck in a pattern of making a lot of money and then losing it because something inside us is saying, "I don't deserve all this." We end up sabotaging ourselves with wrong thinking and a wrong belief system, and no matter how hard we try to break free from this cycle, we can't because we don't have what we need to sustain it.

Ben said this about wholeness: "Third John 2 says, 'Beloved, I wish that you may prosper in all things and be in good health just as your soul prospers.' So in the measure that our soul prospers, everything else in our life will prosper."

This is vital for us to understand. As we learn to demolish the wrong thinking from our lives and receive the healing we need for our soul to become whole, we will begin to see every area of our life prosper.

How To Forgive

Forgiving yourself or someone else is a decision. So how do we forgive? In Luke 17:6, Jesus said we need to deal with unforgiveness like a sycamine tree. Sycamine wood was used to build caskets, which tells us that if we don't deal with bitterness and unforgiveness, it will put us six feet under. Jesus also told us to speak to the sycamine tree. We can't just think about forgiving; we have to use our voice. Say to the unforgiveness in your life, "I'm speaking to you, and I'm telling you to go. I command you to leave my life." You have to speak to it like it's an enemy — because it *is* an enemy — and keep speaking to it until it's dead.

It can feel difficult to forgive someone because when you are wounded by someone, it creates a ditch in your brain, and every time you think of that person, even if you decide to forgive him, your brain will go back to that ditch and you'll feel the pain all over again. And while we as Christians choose to forgive and obey what Jesus has commanded us to do, healing from that wound can be a process. But Philippians 4:8 shows us how to apply healing to that wound. It says:

> **Finally, brethren, whatsoever things are true, whatsoever things are honest, whatsoever things are just, whatsoever things are pure, whatsoever things are lovely, whatsoever things are of good report; if there be any virtue, and if there be any praise, think on these things.**

The Holy Spirit showed this verse to Ben and said, "This is how you heal, not just forgive. This is how you heal." Ben used this verse to think about the person who hurt him and forced his mind to remember what was true about his friend, what good times he shared with him, and what was lovely, pure, and just in their relationship. And once he did, it brought peace and wholeness. What was in disorder was brought back to order. And you can do the same thing too.

STUDY QUESTIONS

Study to shew thyself approved unto God, a workman that needeth not to be ashamed, rightly dividing the word of truth.
— 2 Timothy 2:15

1. In this lesson, Ben described what a stronghold is and how it takes root in your mind. In your own words, describe this process. What happens first? How does it begin to grow? What cements it into place?

2. Why is it important to heal and become whole in your soul? What effect can having a stronghold in your soul have on your life and your relationships?

3. In Second Corinthians 10:5, what Roman weapon does the phrase "taking every thought captive" describe? Why is this important to remember as you are learning to take control of your wrong thinking?

4. From what the "sons of Issachar" shared, what is one way you can start to fight back against your wrong thinking?

PRACTICAL APPLICATION

But be ye doers of the word, and not hearers only, deceiving your own selves.
— James 1:22

1. Are there any strongholds in your life that need to come down? If so, pray and ask the Holy Spirit to reveal to you what is at the root of that stronghold. Once you know what it is, dedicate time each day to spend reading the Bible and spending time with God so He can renew your mind.

2. In the program, Ben shared about how the enemy throws thoughts at us and then tries to convince us they are our own. What thoughts is

he trying to convince you to believe? Are there any lies you are believing about yourself or attaching to your identity?

3. Is there someone in your life that you need to forgive or a wound that you need healing for? Read Philippians 4:8 and pray through this verse while thinking of the person who hurt you. Ask the Holy Spirit to help you remember the things that are true, just, pure, and good about that person.

NOTES

Ben Diaz. *Supernatural Healing of the Soul: Break Free From Toxic Cycles and Unlock Wholeness in Every Area of Your Life.* Shippensburg, PA: Harrison House Publishers, 2025.

LESSON 10

TOPIC

Servants of Fire

SYNOPSIS

In this final lesson of *The Sons of Issachar*, Joseph Z shares from his book *Servants of Fire*. He explains the importance of right-sizing angelic encounters and how to deploy God's heavenly army to minister to our needs. With his balanced approach, Joseph emphasizes the importance of God's Word in activating angels and understanding how they do and do not operate.

We are living in the last of the last days, and it is more important than ever for us as believers to recognize what supernatural help has been made available to us. To shed some light on this subject, the "sons of Issachar" share personal testimonies of angelic help, provision, and intervention, shedding some much-needed understanding on the topic of angels as they look ahead to the role angelic ministry will have in the days to come.

The emphasis of this lesson:

Both the Church and the world deserve to see the supernatural power of God released through angelic ministry in these last days, but it will

require mature believers who are filled with the Word of God, filled with the Spirit, trained, and disciplined to rise to the occasion and activate these fiery servants. If you will study what the Word of God says about angels and pray those biblical commands from your mouth, you will begin to see Heaven's armies dispatched in your life.

Angelic Ministry Should Not Be 'Sensational'

It seems that most people in the Body of Christ don't utilize what supernatural help is available to them. Joseph Z said that often they have some fantastic notion about how angelic ministry works, so they construct their understanding of it on top of the metaphors and cute sayings they hear other people use to describe angels rather than on the Word of God. But to walk on the foundation that God has called us to and access the fullness of what He has provided, we need to look at Scripture to see what His Word has to say about angels and angelic ministry.

When people sensationalize something like angelic encounters, it hurts the testimony of the legitimate. For example, no one sees an angel every five minutes. Now, it shouldn't surprise us when we see an angel, especially in a room where the Bible is taught, because First Peter 1:12 tells us anytime the Word of God is taught angels are there to listen. But someone who claims to see an angel every five minutes is exaggerating and creates confusion around whether legitimate angelic encounters are true or not.

So what should we do to minimize sensationalism in the Church? First, we need to lay the foundation of what the Word of God says about angels. The truth is, many Christians who become mystical in their view of angels fall into deception because they want to, at least in part. They love sensationalism so much and they get so caught up in stories and narratives, wanting an experience so badly, that they compromise what the Bible says and blur the lines to get to that point.

In Colossians 2, the apostle Paul corrected believers for worshiping angels. They had become obsessed with angels, and Paul essentially said to the Colossians, "Guys, you have intruded into things mentally that don't exist." When we are not tethered to the Word of God, we are opening the door for delusion and fantasies that dilute the true power angelic ministry should have in our lives.

Maturity Is Needed in the Body of Christ

Joseph shared that often in the prophetic community sensationalism abounds, but once he found Rick's teachings, they began to bring understanding and order to the wild, sensational encounters he was having. And anyone who has spiritual gifts that lead them to operate in the powerful side of things or in mystical revelation needs to have a firm hold on the Word of God. It will anchor you and ground you as the bedrock of your life.

One issue emerging in our culture is witchcraft. A lot of young people are participating in sorcery and supernatural things that they don't understand, and it's likely because they are not seeing the supernatural power of God in the Church. But the Church is *filled* with the power of God. We have the gifts of the Spirit, the Holy Spirit, and angels that are all over the place in the Church, yet people don't see it. They haven't had their eyes open to see them or understand how the power of God operates in the Church.

Joseph made this powerful statement in the program: "Both the Church and the world deserve to see something. They deserve to see mature believers. They deserve to see people that are so inundated with the Word of God, filled with the Spirit, with discipline, with training, that they begin to rise up to the occasion."

This is why it is so important for you to glean all you can from the teachings in this study guide. The Lord wants to equip you with all you need to stand and rise to the occasion as a mature believer in Christ, but it will take your discipline and faithfulness to study the Word of God and pray in the Spirit to activate these gifts in your life. You are anointed for such a time as this, and as Joseph often says, "On a bad day you're anointed to be the best there is."

Understanding Angelic Intervention

You might be wondering, *What are real angelic encounters like?* Joseph and Rick shared that they have each had real encounters with angels. For Rick, he had two vivid encounters with angels and both times it was unanticipated. He didn't go out looking for them; instead, it was like another realm invaded his life. And this is consistent with each of their encounters. They weren't seeking a spiritual experience, but suddenly an angel appeared and interrupted their lives with a message.

Angels don't respond to us when we cry or beg them to act. They don't respond to whatever religious systems say we should do. Angels are *powerful* and *fierce*, and they only respond to the Word of God.

Joseph said this about activating angels: "I believe when we put the voice of God, which is the written Word of God, in our mouth and we speak it out, that voice comes through into the realm of the spirit and divides those flames of fire [angels], because Hebrews 1 calls them 'those flaming fiery servants that minister to the heirs of salvation.' I also think of Psalm 91, which says angels have hands. They have physical hands that can intervene in the natural."

What examples of angelic intervention do we see in the Bible? When Paul was in prison in Acts 16 and it shook, it is possible that angels put their hands on the ground or grabbed the jail cell and shook it. And when all the believers were interceding for Peter's rescue in Acts 12, an angel "smote" him and woke him up. There were also several angels that intervened at Jesus' resurrection. They rolled the stone away from the tomb and delivered messages to His disciples.

Philip shared this example of angelic intervention in his own life:

> I see angels operate in my life on a regular basis. I remember one time we were at Mardi Gras, and Mardi Gras is like a million people on crack. It is a wild, wild atmosphere, and I don't need to go into anything deeper than that. But I remember it is so packed that there's barely any place to move, and I remember talking to my team.
>
> They said, 'Philip, there's literally no place where we can set up.' I said, 'I've already sent my angels, and they have a perfect spot. It's right in the midst of all the junk.' And sure enough, it was right in front of a strip club, and for some reason that place was untouched and it was enough space. Through that outreach, we saw 1,080 people get saved because the angels had gone ahead of time and they had prepared a spot that no one took.

This is not something unique to Philip or any other minister you've seen in these programs. Angelic intervention and angelic ministry are available to every believer, but many don't take advantage of it because they don't know it exists. That is why it's so important to study what the Word of God says about angels. Once you know what is at your disposal and how to activate it, you will be dangerous to the kingdom of darkness, and you will begin to see the effects of angelic ministry in your life.

Rick added this statement: "There's so much ministry we don't take advantage of because we just don't know. Angels can go for us. They can serve for us. In fact, they're called 'ministers,' and the word 'ministers' is the Greek word *diakonia*, which describes *high-level, trained servants*. It was usually used to describe people who served food and attended to the needs of their masters. The same word is used to describe Jesus at the end of the temptation in the wilderness. The angels came to Him and ministered to Him — the Greek says they came up and *deaconed* Him. They ministered to His needs, they brought Him food, they asked, 'How can I help you?' Angels are really available to minister to us. And when they do, it is the highest level of service."

Common Questions Answered

In this section, we are going to look at some common questions about angels and what the "sons of Issachar" answered in response.

Who commissions angels? Do we commission them or does God?

Joseph answered: "I believe that God is a consuming fire, and if they [angels] are fiery servants, I believe that they were created from the very presence of God. Like they're part of the Lord these ministering spirits. So when the Word of God speaks…when we begin to speak the word of God in faith and it's mixed up in our heart with faith, I believe it activates them because we're doing the will of God. We're speaking what they know."

The next time you ride in a car or board an airplane, you might quote Psalm 91:11, saying, "He shall give His angels charge over me," and when you quote that scripture, you're activating the ministry of angels. Angels are always on hand, but they are not activated unless you speak the Word of God.

Are angels limited by time?

Joseph answered: "I don't know the answer to that, but I know God's outside of time. Here's what I do know: In the book of Revelation when it's talking about John when he fell down to start worshiping that angel, in Revelation 19:10 the angel said, 'See that you do not do that. Worship God for the Spirit of Prophecy is the testimony of Jesus.' And when you look at that picture, I really think angels still in a sense may have free will. But I think they saw what happened to their mutinous brothers to such an extent that when a man would fall down and begin to worship, the angel was like, 'Whoa, whoa. Please don't do that. Lord, you see this guy right here? See me Lord? Yeah, no. I'm not taking any of that. I don't want to be in hell forever or the lake of fire. I think I'll just stand back and say I'm a servant like you.'"

Do angels ever teach or preach?

Rick answered: "In Scripture, angels never teach. They are not teachers and they're not preachers. Teaching and preaching is entrusted to us. But angels do declare. They make announcements, and they make word-for-word verbatim announcements. What they hear, they announce, but they don't have the ability to process and to analyze and to teach and to preach. Those are skills that are uniquely given to the Church.

"In fact, most cults usually can be traced to some kind of angelic teaching…. That's one way you know that it is not right. If you hear that an angel came and gave a teaching, you need to stay away from that."

Can angels provide resources for me like finances and transportation?

Joseph answered: "With those kinds of things…I still believe you've got to do it biblically, which means you are sowing aggressively and you are giving aggressively. There are a lot of ministries that don't sow, but they ask for resources, and I think that's wrong. But when you're a giver, a sower, and you begin to sow the seed and do what the Word of God is saying to do, then you have the authority to stand on that word and then angels will go and do those things. If you're not doing what the Bible says, and you're like, 'Hey! Skippy angel, go do this.' That kind of thing is not going to work for you because you have to do what the Bible says first. That's just how I see it with the Word of God."

Examples of Angelic Ministry

Each of the "sons of Issachar" have stories of when angels intervened to help them and protect them, but here are just a few that were shared in the program.

Joseph said that when he was younger, he was casting demons out of people and a witch began manifesting a demon. She was flopping around, and he didn't know what to do, so he began quoting Psalm 91 and asked for angelic help. Then suddenly the witch was laid flat on the ground. The demon inside her couldn't fight against the invisible angel that pinned her down.

Rick shared that one time he was on a plane he was fairly certain would crash, so he quoted Psalm 91. Then after a series of events, he and the other passengers were delivered from that plane. It was a miracle, and only an angel could have done it.

Gabe said that he and his wife recently rode an elevator up to the sixth floor of their hotel, but instead of the doors opening, they heard a screeching and it proceeded to fall. They looked at each other and said, "Jesus!" and within two seconds the elevator almost paused in time. Then the doors opened, and they were back on the first floor.

Joseph also shared that one time he and his wife Heather were driving down a freeway into what happened to be a tornado and lightning hit the windshield. He yelled, "Jesus!" and all of a sudden, they were out of the storm and everything was fine.

We're living at the end of the age, and we should anticipate angelic ministry. In the book of Revelation, angels are active everywhere even in the Tribulation doing all kinds of things. Rick said this: "I think as the righteous begin to shine more brilliantly, we need to expect portals to open and angelic intervention."

Angels are just standing by waiting to be put to work, and if God gave them to us, we need to know how to use them. We don't need to struggle in our flesh to do things on our own. We don't need to twiddle our thumbs and wonder why no one is coming to help us. We need to activate angelic ministry by speaking the Word of God and to expect these high-level servants to come. Just think of the stories in the Bible where angels fought for the righteous. In Second Kings 19, one angel killed 185,000 Assyrians in one night to protect God's people. That's how it will be when Jesus releases His angels on the earth when He returns and we win the battle of Armageddon.

Last Thoughts About Angels

God has given us angelic ministry for a reason, and we need to know how to use it. Knowing how to activate these "servants of fire" will equip us for the days we're living in and the days ahead. Angels understand whose side we're on and they know the absolute power of the One we serve. They are not confused or troubled, they are just waiting to be activated and put to work. So don't get caught up trying to do everything by yourself. Call on the heavenly messengers God has provided to help you. Put the Word of God in your mouth and watch them go to work on your behalf.

STUDY QUESTIONS

Study to shew thyself approved unto God, a workman that needeth not to be ashamed, rightly dividing the word of truth.
— 2 Timothy 2:15

1. Why is it important to study what the Word of God says about angels versus chasing after an experience? What did the apostle Paul correct the Colossian believers for doing?

2. What is evidence of a real, authentic angelic encounter? How often are these encounters initiated by humans first?

3. In this lesson, Rick said the Greek word for "ministers" describes what? What does this tell us about angelic ministry and what we can expect when we call on angels to help.

4. Who commissions or activates angels, you or God? What do you need to do in order for angels to hear and respond to you?

PRACTICAL APPLICATION

But be ye doers of the word, and not hearers only,
deceiving your own selves.
— James 1:22

1. Have you ever had an angelic encounter in your life? If so, write record your experience. What about it was similar or different than the testimonies shared in this lesson?

2. Have you been stuck in sensational or wrong thinking concerning angels? If so, repent and study what the Word of God says before listening to any more stories from other people. This will keep you grounded and lay a foundation for you to build on as you learn to rightly activate angelic ministry in your own life.

3. Do you regularly activate angels? Why or why not? What impact do you think you would begin to see if you consistently prayed the Word

of God over you and your family? Make a list of two or three scriptures and begin to pray them out loud every day.

NOTES

Joseph Z. *Servant's of Fire — Secrets of the Unseen War and Angels Fighting for You.* Shippensburg, PA: Harrison House Publishers, 2023.

A Prayer To Receive Salvation

If you've never received Jesus as your Savior and Lord, now is the time for you to experience the new life Jesus wants to give you! To receive God's gift of salvation that can be obtained through Jesus alone, pray this prayer from your heart:

> *Jesus, I repent of my sin and receive You as my Savior and Lord. Wash away my sin with Your precious blood and make me completely new. I thank You that my sin is removed, and Satan no longer has any right to lay claim on me. Through Your empowering grace, I faithfully promise that I will serve You as my Lord for the rest of my life.*

If you just prayed this prayer of salvation, you are born again! You are a brand-new creation in Christ! Would you please let us know of your decision by going to **renner.org/salvation**? We would love to connect with you and pray for you as you begin your new life in Christ.

Scriptures for further study: John 3:16; John 14:6; Acts 4:12; Ephesians 1:7; Hebrews 10:19,20; 1 Peter 1:18,19; Romans 10:9,10; Colossians 1:13; 2 Corinthians 5:17; Romans 6:4; 1 Peter 1:3

Notes

CLAIM YOUR FREE RESOURCE!

As a way of introducing you further to the teaching ministry of Rick Renner, we would like to send you FREE of charge his teaching, "How To Receive a Miraculous Touch From God" on CD or as an MP3 download.

In His earthly ministry, Jesus commonly healed *all* who were sick of *all* their diseases. In this profound message, learn about the manifold dimensions of Christ's wisdom, goodness, power, and love toward all humanity who came to Him in faith with their needs.

☑ **YES, I want to receive Rick Renner's monthly teaching letter!**

Simply scan the QR code to claim this resource or go to:
renner.org/claim-your-free-offer

Connect
WITH US!

www.ingramcontent.com/pod-product-compliance
Lightning Source LLC
LaVergne TN
LVHW022324080426
835508LV00041B/2556